Emergency care workers well know that time frequently touches on eternity. Such deeply personal matters are frequently acknowledged but seldom discussed. From his remarkable experience Jeff O'Driscoll discusses that reality in riveting detail. This bravely told autobiographical experience provides that which we all seek: HOPE.

Kirk M. Gilmore, MD
Emergency Physician

Dr. O'Driscoll's account of his many shared experiences through the veil of mortality asks important questions about the meaning and purpose of life. Anyone seeking to enhance or understand their own spiritual gifts will be challenged and enlightened by his journey. The narrative style is very accessible while at the same time deeply layered with wisdom that bears repeated reading and reflection.

Marv Curtis
Fly Fisherman & Raconteur

Not Yet

Near-Life Experiences
& Lessons Learned

Jeff O'Driscoll, MD

DEDICATION

Stanton K O'Driscoll

CONTENTS

ACKNOWLEDGMENTS

Thank you to Jeffery C. Olsen
for twenty years of friendship and encouragement.

FOREWORD

Trusted friends are rare and wonderful. Having lost a few of my best, young and unexpectedly, I've learned to never take for granted the opportunity to laugh, cry and share with a vulnerability that makes each moment real.

I lost half my family and half my body in a tragic auto accident. In an instant, my life broke into two parts: before the wreck and after. Yet life's most powerful segment came in between. Those minutes, hours, weeks and months, when my life hung in the balance, my spirit roamed from this realm to the next. I experienced what follows this world, only to return and continue my journey here.

My near-death experience sustained me through the grief, shock and bereavement of losing so much, but the path was still difficult. Despite the beauty of traveling beyond the mortal veil, it was difficult to know who to trust, whom to discuss it with and how much to share. I never imagined that my emergency physician, a stranger, would become one of a few people I could really open up to.

Jeff O'Driscoll was always willing to listen, without judgment, as I wandered the path, picking up the pieces and attempting to make sense of what had shattered my world. I tasted unconditional love on the other side. I knew the sum from experience, but I wanted to piece together the equation. I wanted to see clearly how it all added up. Being able to speak openly and share personal aspects of what I had experienced, and continue to experience, with an unbiased medical doctor made me feel incredibly safe while exploring my newly awakened perspective.

One glorious takeaway from my near-death experience is my knowledge that life truly never ends, and yet, what really matters is today. My near-death experience is not nearly as important as my Life Experience and what I came here to learn in every sacred moment of the eternal continuum of now. Little things are big things when we see the synchronicity and divine order of life. Having a trusted friend who 'gets it' is a gift I will always honor. I respect how Jeff O'Driscoll opens up in the following pages and expounds on what he has learned and experienced. One need not die and return to connect with our Divine Source. Jeff is proof of that. As an ER Physician, he deals with death often, but how he chooses to live makes him a true healer.

Jeffery C. Olsen
Near-Death Experiencer

PREFACE

It's strange to contemplate sharing my deeply personal experiences with the world. I'm not inclined to talk about myself. I'm even less inclined to talk to strangers about my personal experiences. Jeff Olsen would quickly confirm. He's been prying fragments from my past for over twenty years. He's allowed me to share at my pace, always providing a safe zone, free from judgment or pressure. I've tried to provide him the same. We've shared a lot.

Jeff was reluctant to share his experiences. He told them to me, sometimes in great detail, but it took him fifteen years to publish his first book, *I Knew Their Hearts*. His second book, *Beyond Mile Marker 80*, followed two years later in 2014. He's now spoken widely about his near-death experiences (NDEs), and he's invited me repeatedly to join him. Until recently I'd declined. I've had spiritual experiences—*Near-Life Experiences*, as I like to call them—but I haven't shared them publicly.

I met Jeff in the emergency department in Salt Lake City, Utah, on the night of his car accident. He was unconscious and badly injured. I was just one of the emergency physicians in the ER that night. I was in the room but not his physician.

I also met Tamara, Jeff's wife, in the trauma room. She'd died at the scene and left her body in southern Utah. She'd come to watch over her husband. Sometimes I think she came to introduce us. She knew we'd become friends. I'd soon know we'd share a future.

I'm perfectly comfortable with NDEs and shared-death experiences (SDEs). After 25 years in and out of the ER, I've witnessed and experienced quite enough spiritual phenomena to know first-hand. When I say spiritual, I mean near-the-veil, when the boundary between mortality and eternity becomes indistinct, when I enjoy a portion of that which exists beyond my mortal senses. And when I say spirit, I mean that eternal portion of a soul, whether in the body or out. Many people use many words for such experiences based on their history and beliefs. I'll use my words; you can substitute the words most comfortable for you.

People ask me about Jeff's medical condition. For me, that's not the question. His physical healing, while miraculous, was not the miracle. Focusing on Jeff's medical condition instead of his NDE is like focusing on a travel brochure while flying at low altitude through the Grand Canyon. Jeff's physical recovery serves only a small part of his story. His is not a medical story. The medical situation was just the milieu in which the spiritual story flourished. Maybe I feel this way because I'm a doctor. I don't find the medical aspects of NDEs particularly unusual or intriguing. I find the medical aspects a distraction from what matters most.

I met Tamara after her death. I accepted Jeff's NDE. We've now been friends for over twenty years and continue to help one another understand our spiritual experiences. That's the story.

I won't attempt to define NDEs or discuss the medical science to justify them. Instead, I'll share how near-life experiences have changed my life and my understanding of life. For me, that's the story.

NDEs happen quickly; understanding them takes time. When I met Jeff, I finally realized one of the reasons for the experiences I'd had previous to our friendship. Very early in our relationship, I realized some of my experiences were to help Jeff understand his. Some experiences are for our personal benefit; some are to share. Ten years after his accident, while visiting the scene of his crash for the first time, Jeff was told to write his experiences and others would heal. Ten more years passed before I received similar impressions.

Recently Jeff left the security of his profession to pursue his passion—to follow his heart. He co-created @ONE (www.atONEnow.com), an organization dedicated to harmonizing the spiritual and scientific aspects of NDEs while giving people a safe place to explore and share. When Jeff told me about his plans, my feelings about sharing began to change. Twenty years ago, on the day we first spoke, I had premonitions about our shared future. That future is now.

I recently joined Jeff to speak publicly for the first time about some of my experiences. It felt good. I'm still anxious about exposing so much, but sharing finally feels right. I've come to learn the universe gently coaxes people into the right time and place. This book is my first attempt to share in print.

Not Yet

1

NOT YET

Two words came into my mind at one of the darkest periods of my life. They came into my heart more than my mind. I felt them more than heard them. I experienced them more than felt them. I understood the message. It seemed merciless and brutal. I wept.

All I wanted was an end to the blackness. I'd asked. My otherworldly answer was, "Not yet." As painful as it was, I now understand the wisdom. It took years.

Too often I ask for the wrong things. I ask innocently, naïvely, sincerely, but for the wrong things. Had I received what I'd asked, everything I experienced thereafter would have been lost. I would not be who I am now.

2

TAMARA

For more than twenty-five years, it's been my sacred privilege
as an emergency physician to greet souls who are entering
this world and bid adieu to those who are leaving. Occasionally I
encounter one who hovers between worlds, not sure whether to
stay or go.

Birth and death can be routine, almost mechanical events.
Sometimes, however, witnessing those miracles and partaking of
them surpasses all earthly joy and all the science taught in medical
school. When unseen factors align, I meet ancient souls
embarking on a new phase of existence. They're invariably
overwhelmed with love and gratitude. They're always grateful.

Late in my shift on March 31, 1997, Rachel grabbed me by the
arm. She was a perpetually calm nurse, now with an urgent
expression. It sounds odd to non-ER people, but ER people
seldom walk or talk with an outward appearance of urgency. They

2

may feel it; but they seldom show it. Too much urgency in an ER makes people nervous. Despite the often-urgent needs of patients, ER people tend to move in a calm, deliberate manner. So Rachel's tone caught my attention.

"She's here," she said. "You've gotta come to the trauma room."

"Who's here?" I asked. "What are you talking about?"

"His wife. She's here."

Everybody in the department knew a trauma patient had arrived. We'd been warned far in advance. We knew about Jeff Olsen's automobile crash in southern Utah, though we did not yet know his name. We knew about his visit to the local emergency department prior to his air transport to Salt Lake City. We knew his wife and 14-month-old son had died at the scene, and that his seven-year-old son had been transported to our neighboring children's hospital. The transferring facility wasn't just communicating morbid information for the sake of speaking; knowing that someone died in a crash tells you something about the magnitude of the impact and energy absorbed by those who survived. Sometimes that information is important in providing care. We'd heard a preliminary report of Jeff's extensive injuries and the overhead announcement of his arrival. Rachel had been in the trauma suite and seen him arrive. Now she was tugging on my arm.

"She's there," she said. "C'mon."

I finally gave way to her insistence as I realized what she was saying. Prior conversations in more relaxed circumstances had primed me for her assertions. She'd experienced numerous spiritual phenomena in the past. Some of her experiences, as she'd shared them privately, had brought me to tears. I'd had my own experiences. We'd discussed some at length. That Rachel had experienced Tamara's presence in the trauma suite did not surprise me; that I believed what she was saying did not surprise her. We quickened our pace as she spoke.

I had no responsibility for Jeff's medical care. That's one reason I saw and heard what I did. When I'm too busy being a doctor—when I'm too busy seeing with my eyes and hearing with my ears, trying to keep someone alive—I may completely miss the profound and eternal around me.

Another emergency physician, along with a trauma surgeon, residents, nurses, and others, had all arrived in the trauma suite prior to Jeff and had immediately initiated his care when he arrived. I'd been blithely engaged in other duties when Rachel approached. Now I was simply an observer.

In the trauma suite I saw the usual army of professionals surrounding a gurney. Bits of an unconscious and battered body were visible through the cracks between personnel. I saw the usual flurry of activity and heard the hum of voices: vital signs, the tail end of a report from the transport team, orders, acknowledgments, tentative plans. Almost as quickly, however, the sounds all faded into silence, like a television show with the sound turned off. People's lips still moved—they could still hear one another—but the room fell silent for me. Even Rachel's voice was gone. A tingle—almost a vibration—began in the center of my soul and radiated outward to the tip of each digit. I felt the hair on my arms and neck stand at attention.

The treatment area was large, with an elevated ceiling and a mirrored observation room that looked down on the scene for teaching purposes. Tamara stood high above my right shoulder and about ten feet away, about halfway between Jeff and I. We'd never met, but I knew her. She calmly surveyed the room, sometimes looking toward me, sometimes toward her severely injured spouse. She had a pleasant countenance and a warm, welcoming disposition. She had long, wavy, blonde hair.

I walked to the gurney and looked at Jeff for the first time. I looked at his badly injured legs. People moved around me, all doing their respective tasks. I had no tasks. I was free to take in the experience, keenly aware of Tamara's continued surveillance over my right shoulder. I may have felt for a pulse in Jeff's left foot; I don't remember for sure. I knew his popliteal artery had been jeopardized by his knee injury. The window for vascular intervention was rapidly closing. His prolonged extrication, previous ER visit in southern Utah, and his air transport, had all chewed away at that critical window of time. His leg, as important as it was, couldn't be the first priority. Before anyone could save his leg, they first had to save his life.

I recall saying to myself, or to Rachel, "He's going to lose the leg." I just knew.

That was about the extent of the medical care I provided to Jeff. I may have consulted with other doctors or done something more—trauma care is a team sport—but I was not his primary doctor and did little, if anything, for his medical benefit.

I don't recall what Tamara said to me in the trauma suite, looking down from her elevated position. Though facing toward Jeff, I could see her behind me. I could see her as clearly behind me as I could see him in front. I could see in every direction at the same time and take it all in more efficiently than if I'd been focusing on a single spot. It's been more than twenty years, and I've rarely spoken of it, but I remember that part clearly.

Tamara may not have said anything at all. Whether she spoke through the silence or communicated without words, I remember quite clearly her expressions of pure gratitude. She was grateful for the team and all they were doing. She was grateful to me for being aware of her. My overall impression was that she was a grateful person and would express her appreciation to each individual if she were able to do so. In that moment, to borrow a phrase I would later hear Jeff use, *I knew her heart.*

Tamara knew at that moment that Jeff would live—that he *should* live, and that there were things for him yet to do in this life. And I knew it with her. It didn't come as some profound revelation or grand mystic truth being pushed upon me. It felt more like common knowledge hanging in the ether, available to any spirit willing to listen. It was like the first twinklings of dawn announcing to anyone willing to open their eyes that another day was approaching. In my experience, that's the way spiritual knowledge feels; even when it's new, it's not a surprise. It feels more like a confirmation than a revelation.

I love such moments because everything reorders. Nothing trivial or temporal matters. In those moments, I see souls as they are, without the filters that incline us to separate people into groups and label individuals who are different from ourselves.

Suddenly I see everyone as alike and I love them all, including myself—something that is difficult for me to do when I'm in the trappings of mortality. I love such moments. I wish I had more of them, except that such experiences make it hard for me to find contentment in this world.

In my characteristically cryptic journal entry that night, I referred to the whole encounter as "an interesting experience." My entries tend to be brief and understated. Too often I write at the end of a long day, when I'm tired and thinking more about getting to bed than recording details or emotions. "I could feel her presence and she thanked me for what I had done for her husband," I wrote. Had it been my first such experience, I might have written more. In retrospect, I wish I had. Knowing me, what I wrote said a lot: "It was powerful."

Looking back, I wonder if Tamara might have been thanking me in advance for what would yet transpire. I wonder, too, if she's been in and out of my life since.

3

LIFE

While **I was** meeting Tamara, Jeff Olsen was exploring the universe. Geographically, he wandered mostly nearby, in the halls and rooms of the hospital; spiritually, he spanned eternity, taking it in as only a spirit could. He'd later tell me much of his experience. The moment I heard fragments, I knew. As clearly as I'd known Tamara's heart, I would know Jeff's. But that was still weeks away. My first real conversation with Jeff wouldn't come until he was out of the hospital. He first had to get well enough to talk.

A lot might be said of Jeff's near-death experience (NDE) or the shared-death experience (SDE) I'd enjoyed with Tamara. Volumes have been written about NDEs. People have debated definitions and argued about their validity. Writers and speakers vary on terminology and even vacillate on the use of the hyphen. I won't attempt to settle any of those issues. I'm not even certain

I'm using the terms correctly. I'm simply sharing a few personal experiences.

I think "near-death" and "shared-death" terminology is unfortunate. It implies such experiences are associated only with death. I know firsthand they may come independent of death or dying. In fact, similar experiences can be powerfully associated with birth. The terminology also suggests the NDE recipient only comes *near* death, without dying. Many who have passed through such experiences would argue they were, indeed, quite dead. I suspect their physicians would agree. And I doubt that debating the definitions of death would change anyone's mind.

My twinge of discomfort about the terminology also stems from my personal encounters and from my simple understanding of birth, life, and death. I think of it this way: the boundary between mortality and eternity—a boundary often referred to as a veil—is drawn back at birth and death, allowing spirits to pass between realms of existence. If I'm near the veil—spiritually near, that is—a portion of eternal glory splashes through and onto me.

So why don't more people see and hear all these spirits coming and going in the ER? In my experience, it's because we are wrapped in a veil of flesh that impairs our sight and muffles our hearing, and because our preoccupations with the things of this world block our spiritual receptiveness. Spirits are very near during birth and death, but the profound joy experienced when a child arrives and the deep sorrow experienced when a loved leaves, consume our attention. The emotional extremes of mortality leave little room for spiritual awareness.

Imagine yourself in a darkened room full of people. It's not black. You can move around and interact. It's just subdued, the colors muted. Two heavy curtains hang floor-to-ceiling and wall-to-wall, one on your right, and one on your left. Beyond the curtains is a glorious inviting light. Now imagine a single slit in the center of each curtain. Every time a soul draws back the curtain on your left to enter the room, or draws back the curtain on your right to leave the room, some of that brilliant light spills into the darkness around you. The closer you are to the opening, the more light you experience before the curtain falls closed.

Sometimes it is drawn back far enough, or held open long enough, for you to glimpse further into the light, to see people and places. And you're deeply disappointed when the curtain again falls shut.

In my analogy, mortality falls between the curtains of our mortal bodies. On our left is birth, and on our right, death. We set aside a portion of our glory to be here, to learn and experience and grow. The light and glory spills into this realm as souls pass through the veil. Sometimes souls (or spirits or beings) are coming, and sometimes they're going. Occasionally they hover between. Once in a while, a person from either side draws back the veil without passing through, giving a glimpse of eternity independent of birth or death. In each of these scenarios, when we experience the light, we stand a little nearer to the glorious life that once was ours and will be again. For that reason, I call them *Near-Life Experiences.*

We are glorious beings, too often unaware, wrapped in the veil that is our mortal body. Parting the veil happens in its most profound way when we enter and leave our body through birth and death. Sometimes, however, our spirits see and hear and comprehend without leaving the body.

> Our birth is but a sleep and a forgetting;
> The Soul that rises with us, our life's Star,
> Hath had elsewhere its setting
> And cometh from afar;
> Not in entire forgetfulness,
> And not in utter nakedness,
> But trailing clouds of glory do we come
> From God, who is our home[1]

I love William Wordsworth's imagery and insight. He goes on to describe how "heaven lies about us in our infancy" and how it comes to "fade into the light of common day." Eventually we

---

[1] "Ode on Intimations of Immortality from Recollections of Early Childhood," William Wordsworth, 1770 – 1850.

forget the glories we've known and the "imperial palace whence [we] came and . . . [our] soul's immensity."

I believe Wordsworth's sequence is accurate because of my daughters. They told me about encounters with divine beings when they were still quite young. They were unembarrassed and matter-of-fact in their descriptions. Their ventures into the light and glory faded over time, and now neither of them remembers those encounters.

We can't prevent the light from fading as we move into this plane. One of the reasons we come is to live for a time away from the constant glory. Our glory is subdued as we are clothed in mortality to enter this realm. Even here, however, there are things we can do to enjoy more light.

I didn't know when I met Tamara that Jeff was having an NDE. I didn't know enough to describe my time with Tamara as an SDE. For me, it was just another shift in the ER. It wasn't an isolated event. I'd been an emergency physician at a level-one trauma center for several years by then. In and out of the department, and before I was a physician, I'd had enough such experiences to lose count. I've had many more since.

I can't explain why the time has come for me to share. I've seldom spoken of my spiritual experiences, and it's never seemed right until now. Most spiritual encounters are sacred and deserve to be handled with discretion. If I speak too often or too indiscriminately, I fear I may sever my connection with the source. However, some experiences are given to me personally; others are given to share. If I fail to share the latter, I fail in my stewardship. But I have to share at the right time and to the right people and with the right sensitivities. I'm no authority on the topic; I'm just a guy with a story. You're under no obligation to accept anything I share, and I'm under no obligation to defend it.

After our brief initial encounter, Jeff left the emergency department, probably to go to the OR, though I don't recall for certain. As wonderful as the experience had been, I'd had others. I had no reason to think this one would be different. I didn't expect to see Jeff again. I finished my shift and went home.

4

STAN

Things were different before June 18, 1973. I didn't realize how different until my mother told me more than twenty years later. Even then, I had to pry it from her. I thought I'd passed through my brother's death unscathed. I was eleven when he died in a farm accident; he was fifteen. We'd been close. We'd hiked, camped and shared a horse. (At that age, we couldn't afford two.) Stan gave me my first beer and my first chew of tobacco, but we don't say those things in front of my mother. At age ten, I thought something called chewing tobacco must be for—well, what else?—chewing. That first pinch of Copenhagen made my head spin and my stomach rumble. I nearly fell off the horse. Stan laughed and laughed.

On another occasion, Stan and I were out with our brother, Dean, and our cousin Dave. Dean and Dave were both between Stan and me in age. We all went ding-dong-ditching late one night—knocking on doors and running away—in Morgan, Utah. Ding-dong-ditching is pretty much the same in the city as in the country, with one major exception. In the country, you don't knock on the same door twice. We were about to learn that.

We knocked on one door and hid across the street to watch. No answer. Leaving Dean and Dave safely in the bushes, Stan and I headed back to the door to compound our late-night disturbance. Stan began rapping on the door, only to have it open suddenly, revealing a man and a shotgun on the other side. It was one of those moments when you take in every detail in an instant: his black and gray chest hair peeking out around his wife-beater T-shirt and extending onto his shoulders and neck, his six-pack that had long ago evolved into a keg, his fleshy fingers wrapped around the gun. He wasn't smiling.

We leapt the front steps and landed half way down the walk as the beer-belly with the scattergun spewed a string of expletives and stepped onto his porch. We didn't look back. All I could see of Stan was his elbows and heels as I tried to keep up. It was hard to run because we were laughing through our terror. We must have run half a mile before we collapsed into a ditch near the road and laughed ourselves to tears. Dean and Dave came along thirty minutes later, after the man finally went back into his house. They weren't laughing. Stan tried to help them see the humor but something about that shotgun didn't amuse them. Stan found the funny in every situation. After our encounter with the Rambo wannabe, we called it a night.

Being the oldest, Stan was, of course, infallible. I believed every word he said until one day when he tried to tell me about sex. "No way," I said, shaking my ten-year-old head and warping my eyebrows in disgust. He offered a reaffirming nod and a crooked grin, but I still wasn't buying it. We moved to a different topic. In my eyes, Stan could do no wrong. I lost something the day he tipped the tractor over, but I had no idea how much.

My mother informed me decades later that she'd always known where I was before June 18 because she could hear me singing. After Stan died, I stopped singing. I don't remember the singing, or stopping, but she does. The experience must have affected me in some primal way because I could never remember the date of his death. I remembered the details of the day—what I saw, what I heard, what I felt, the anguished scream of my mother when she heard the news—but I couldn't remember the date. I only remember it now because I happened to notice, while staring at Stan's headstone as an adult, that the doleful date falls half way between my wedding anniversary and my youngest daughter's birthday. I loved my brother; I still do. There must have been some deep pathologic reason why I couldn't remember that date.

Several years ago, my wife and I spoke about buying a new house. There was nothing wrong with the house we lived in (we still live in it), but, after visiting a colleague in her fancy new mansion, we contemplated getting something nicer. I remember thinking I didn't want a house I could get emotionally attached to. I didn't want a house I cared about losing. In fact, I didn't want anything in my life, object or person, which could hurt me by leaving.

I jerked my head slightly and blinked as the thought stormed through my mind, like I couldn't believe my own contemplations. "Wait a minute," I said out loud. "That's not normal."

Over a period of months, I researched my reluctance to attach myself to people or things. Without seeing a professional, I concluded I had some measure of attachment disorder. Fear had constructed a protective barrier between me and the fullness of human emotion. I think it stemmed from the loss of my brother and an unconscious decision to never allow myself to be hurt like that again.

Stan has visited me several times since he died. Sometimes I know it's him. Sometimes I conclude without knowing. He visited more frequently in the year I met Jeff and Tamara. Older brothers are older brothers, even when they're dead.

5

RACHEL

I **met Rachel** in 1996, about six months before she dragged me into the trauma room to meet Tamara. I don't recall the exact circumstances, but we felt a connection. She soon came to meet my wife and visit in our home. We talked for four hours. She wore a bright countenance and an inviting smile. She spoke comfortably about her spiritual experiences and helped me feel a little more comfortable about sharing some of mine. Before she left, she asked me for a special prayer on her behalf. I readily agreed. Rachel had come during a dark and difficult time in my life. She asked for help, but I later concluded she'd been sent to give help more than receive it.

Late in December, just a few months after Rachel and I met, I came home from a long shift in the ER. I was tired and ready for a rest. Just as I settled into a soft chair, I recognized the pained cry of seven-year-old Jacob. I knew from the tone of his voice he was injured. Parents know. I looked at my wife rather unsympathetically and said, "He'll just have a scar. I'm not going back to the ER tonight."

A few moments later, Jacob's older brother ascended the stairs with a bloody boy in his arms. I gave Jacob a hug and lifted the edge of a towel to assess the gaping wound in his left eyebrow. He and his brother had been Sumo wrestling. The pillows under their shirts served as fulcrums, turning their bodies into top-heavy levers. When their bellies collided at full speed, Jacob flew around the room until his head struck some unforgiving surface. He and I were soon in the ER.

One glance conveyed Jacob's anxiety. It fully eclipsed his physical pain. I felt it—the anxiety, the pain, everything. I experienced a perfect flow of empathy.

I'd sutured hundreds of lacerations, including several on my own children, but the experience that night was more than a mere wound repair. It proved profoundly instructive. It became a paradigm shift in my relationship with Heaven.

As an emergency physician, I knew what was coming to Jacob, how long it would last, and what the scar would look like if the wound were left unsutured. I had all that perspective from experience. Jacob had only pain, anxiety, and the fear of the unknown, all held in-check only by his trust in me and his knowledge that I loved him.

I reassured Jacob as I proceeded to anesthetize his wound. I knew the first needle was the most painful. I knew how brief that pain would be. He was almost in tears when he looked up and said, "Please, Dad, don't hurt me anymore."

I still get a lump in my throat whenever I recall that moment, perhaps because it struck so close to home. I'd uttered the same plea three years before. His words reflected the sentiments of untold millions who plead with Heaven to be delivered from their pain. Meanwhile, an infinitely loving Creator knows what my spiritual scars will look like and how much angst and regret they will ultimately cause if I refuse the sometimes painful but healing touch. My well-intended petitions are often so shortsighted. Though the words may vary according to one's religious background, I imagine the following dialogue between a loving God and a naïve supplicant:

"Please, Father, don't hurt me any more."

"But this is part of what you're on earth to experience. I'm helping you."

"Yes, I know, but please don't hurt me any more."

"Trust me. I love you. There's purpose in this. I'll help you through it."

"Yes, yes, I know. But this is just too difficult. Just trust me this one time, Father. Please, make it stop."

I'm a prayerful person. Sometimes I ponder or meditate or engage in dialogue with my inner self. Sometimes I pray silently as I care for a patient, pleading that I might discern the correct diagnosis and treatment. Sometimes I pray vocally when no other mortal is there to listen. Sometimes I pray while running or riding my bike, or sometimes on my knees. Regardless of how we picture our Creator or the gender of the pronouns we use, there is a form of prayer for every circumstance.

My experience with Jacob that night changed my life and my prayers. I try now to exercise greater trust in a Divine Being who loves me more than I love myself and who has purpose in the difficult experiences I'm invited to pass through. Rather than trying to inform God of the facts, to help him better understand my needs and see things my way, I feel inclined to acknowledge the omniscience of Heaven and the perfect benevolence necessary to customize the healing of my wounds. Rather than asking for such experiences to be taken away, I strive to ask: What should I learn? How can I be strengthened? How can I use this experience to help others?

It took years of darkness and pain to prepare me for Jacob's request. I could not have appreciated its significance had it come sooner in my life.

Sheila wanted to be with her son while he was being sutured, but she stayed home with the other four kids. Our daughters were just three and five years old, hardly ideal for a family visit to the ER. Next to the suture table, compassionately holding Jacob's hand, sat Rachel. A single mother filled with compassion, she understood his request. I was glad she was there. Later, during one of my most difficult times, Rachel asked me to fast and pray for her. I asked, of all the people in her life, why she would trust me with such a thing. "Because the Lord has allowed me to see who you are," she said, rather matter-of-factly. She said it as if everyone could see into heaven the way she could. "I would trust you with my life."

Rachel blessed my life when she dragged me into the trauma room to meet Tamara. She would bless me again when she dragged me back into Jeff's life a month later.

6

JEFFERY

I **hadn't seen** Jeff in almost a month. To be honest, I'd hardly thought of him. I'd had no reason to believe I'd see him again. As far as I knew—and this was only because Rachel had kept tabs on his progress—he was on the mend. The only reason Jeff and I reconnected was Rachel.

A few weeks after Jeff's horrible accident, Rachel approached me at work. She insisted I go with her to see Jeff and tell him about our encounter with Tamara. To say I was reluctant would be an understatement. Ambivalence would be a good word, though I am embarrassed to admit feeling it. I wasn't inclined to share my personal experience with a complete stranger. It had taken weeks, in tiny increments, to warm up to Rachel enough to share, and my connection to her had been faster than most. I've rarely been quick to share. The comfort I enjoyed with Rachel stemmed largely from the fact that she'd had similar experiences—visions too sacred for me to describe—and we understood one another.

There are people around you who have visions and dreams, who see spirits and speak to them; they just don't talk about it. There's a collective notion that spiritual phenomena are rare or imagined. Neither is the case. Some people want more; some want less. I've been on both sides of that: sometimes wanting more, sometimes less.

I knew nothing about Jeff's spiritual proclivities. I was convinced that sharing would benefit neither him nor me. But Rachel demanded I go. She was a hard person to refuse, and for that I'm grateful.

On Sunday, 27 April, Rachel and I walked into the university hospital and headed to the elevator. In the weeks since we'd met, Jeff had slogged through the horrors of the medical system, including a transfer from our trauma center as mandated by his ever-benevolent insurance company. He'd endured several surgeries, including the amputation of his left leg. In addition to his orthopedic injuries, his lungs were badly contused, his chest wall severely traumatized, and his bowel ruptured. He appeared to have lost a lot of weight. He was a living petri dish waiting for an infection.

When Rachel and I walked into Jeff's room, we were unaware of the spiritual experiences he'd later write about. Perhaps he and I were equally unenthused about sharing our sacred moments with strangers. His expression projected apprehension.

Jeff and I let Rachel carry the weight of the conversation. She seemed more comfortable than either of us. We each nodded at appropriate times and dropped a few innocuous comments as needed to be polite. If fact, I was so closed-mouthed, I left Jeff with two complete misimpressions: First, he thought I had some significant role in his medical care; and, second, he'd later write that I'd felt Tamara's presence but not seen her. I saw her. Let me be clear about that. Let me add, however, that most people use the word *see* to describe what mortal eyes process. Spiritual eyes *see* things differently. They don't just see or hear; they experience. If words come, they are accompanied by pages or volumes of understanding, all in an instant. If no words are used, the knowledge flows unimpeded, soul-to-soul, as if the spirits had no bodies to impede their communication. I experienced Tamara and received the message she shared. I knew her. I regret not making that clear to Jeff the first day we spoke. Ironically, now that he and I speak the same spiritual language, we use far fewer words to communicate.

Rachel told Jeff about our encounter with Tamara. They both wept. I don't recall what he or I said. I do recall my feelings. As they visited, I found myself increasingly distracted by a growing premonition. Near the end of our conversation, the feeling had become so strong it led me to a conclusion. My visit with Jeff that day was virtually inconsequential save one thing: it linked us to the next twenty years. I knew then that we would become good friends and that there was purpose in our shared future.

Later that day, I wrote in my journal, "What impressed me more than the experiences we had shared, were the strong impressions I repeatedly felt. There are significant things I will yet share with him." Looking back, it strikes me that my unusual and specific feelings were not about what Jeff would share with me, but about what I would share with him. I couldn't have known how true that impression would be.

Jeff appreciated our visit enough to call me two weeks later and thank me for coming. That I'd left him my number bespeaks the strong connection I'd felt.

7

JEFFREY

I'm not fond of writing about myself, but I suppose it's
necessary if I'm going to talk about Jeff Olsen's story and the
beginnings of our friendship. When we met, I was 35 years old,
just two years older than Jeff. We'd both been married close to
ten years. Sheila and I were raising five kids, three boys and two
girls. Our youngest would soon be five. Marriage and kids were
just a sliver of what Jeff and I had in common and what would
shape our shared friendship.

After Stan died, Dean looked out for me. He was just one year
ahead of me in school and always provided the good example I
seldom followed. I'd often walk through the front door of the
church with my family and out the back door with my friends. I
couldn't abide being indoors on a beautiful, inviting day. Sitting
on a grassy ridge in the mountains behind the church, chewing
sunflower seeds and reading horoscopes, proved far more

appealing than the interminable tedium of church.

My sister, Michelle, was a few years younger than I. With Stan no longer there to protect her, she endured my relentless teasing.

My school years weren't easy for my parents. Mom and Dad proved heroic in their efforts to see me graduate. I think I was acting out the grab-life-by-the-horns-and-hang-on attitude I'd learned from Stan. Let's just say I was a challenge. My poor mother took far too many disappointing phone calls from school administrators, most often because I'd been in a fight. Dad usually got the bad news from Mom when he'd come home from work. He probably dreaded coming home, wondering what might be waiting.

I grew up in a traditional family with traditional values. My mother was a great cook and a true saint. Every day, when Dad came home from the office, we all sat down to a home-cooked family meal complete with dessert. Our garden, orchard, and livestock, provided fresh food in season and home-preserved food at other times of the year. The nightly dinner tradition made Stan's empty seat at the table all the more noticeable.

Jeff and I might have been friends growing up had we ever met. We are about the same age and shared a heritage in neighboring counties of rural Utah: football, rodeo, hard work, love of the land, and livestock. We might have disagreed on two points. First, when it came to rodeo, he rode bareback broncs; I rode bulls. I think I would have eventually converted him, though he might disagree. Second, he spelled his name wrong: Jeffery. I spelled mine correctly: Jeffrey.

People who know me now find it hard to believe I was ever too talkative. In junior high, my disruptive behavior led to one of those disappointing phone calls. My father offered a thoughtful solution. He gave me a small notebook and an assignment. I was to write down almost everything I said. To be polite and respectful, I could respond to direct questions and return greetings without writing. Everything else was to be recorded in the notebook. I could go ahead and say it; I just had to also write it down.

The effect was amazing and almost immediate. I soon learned

that most of what I said wasn't worth writing, and certainly not worth being accountable for. I learned to speak more judiciously and to think before I spoke.

A few years later, I applied the notebook principle to my spiritual life. I was serving a two-year mission for The Church of Jesus Christ of Latter-day Saints (the Mormons) in England at the time. If the notebook could change my speech habits so quickly and effectively, I thought it might help with other behaviors, like ingratitude, impatience, and being too *laissez-faire* about my spiritual growth. I thought spirituality was a gift that came and went as it pleased without any input from the people it touched. I've since learned otherwise.

In my notebook, I jotted frequent memos of things I wanted to remember, to contemplate further, to eliminate from my life or to improve. Sometimes it was a question or a misstep I wanted to correct, sometimes an experience I wanted to remember gratefully. I soon learned that when I pulled out my notebook at night, I had a well-prepared agenda for prayer.

As I said in a previous chapter, I believe in prayer. I believe in meditation and quiet contemplation and communing with the Divine. I believe the Universe can influence and instruct us. I believe I can converse with my Creator regardless of the language or circumstance. For me, prayer, in its many forms, is simply an exercise in penetrating the veil. When I labor at the veil, I see and hear and feel what otherwise goes unnoticed.

If an agenda for prayer sounds irreverent, I suggest it's quite the opposite. The most important meetings in business and politics are almost invariably benefitted by an agenda. If I attended such a meeting, I'd come prepared. If I initiated such a meeting, I'd be expected to have an agenda. Failing to do so might be considered arrogant or disrespectful. We can, of course, pray at any time. We can drop in, so to speak, just to say hi or to have a casual conversation, but appearing before my Maker with a well-thought-out agenda demonstrated my commitment to the process.

When I first opened my notebook during prayer, I experienced an unanticipated consequence. In addition to helping me be more prepared, it helped me be more receptive. When I listened—something I do too seldom during prayer—I was given something to write. Sometimes it was encouragement, sometimes chastisement, sometimes an assignment. If the process sounds irreverent, imagine yourself walking out of a government or business meeting without notes, and then going back a month later to ask the same question again because you've forgotten the answer. Imagine asking the person you most respect to repeat what they've said because you didn't write it down and you forgot. As absurd as it sounds, we often do just that in prayer.

Why would we practice baseball, piano, sculpting, or medicine while expecting to get spiritual issues right the first time? We need practice. At least I do. Sometimes people ask me about spiritual feelings. I don't know why, but sometimes they ask me about feelings they've had or what they can do to find a spiritual connection. I don't have any special knowledge, and it's different for everyone, but I share with him or her what works for me. I just try to point them toward the light.

When I help someone recognize spiritual promptings, I take them to a sacred place—someplace quiet where they feel at ease, someplace beautiful or inspiring or otherwise special—and talk to them about sacred things. Almost invariably, they feel something beyond the common. It may be only an inkling, but it's a start. When they feel it, I encourage them to register the feeling and remember it, and when it comes again, to act. In other words, I tell them to practice. Babies roll over, then they crawl, then they stand, then they walk, then they run. Eventually they may dance.

If we would walk with the Divine, we have to start somewhere. Often, it's a subtle feeling or just a question. The next time you get that feeling, pause and be quiet. Take a slow deep breath and wait. Ponder the situation and ask why? Be prepared to write down the answer and to act. Practice makes perfect. You will grow into it. I promise.

Let me share just two notebook experiences: the first humorous, the second more sacred.

More than a decade into using my notebook, I came across some interesting information about an early American folk practice of using prayer rods. Documents suggest people had rods that somehow assisted them in prayer. For example, they might hold the rod vertically and ask a question. When they released the rod, if it fell one direction the answer was yes; if it fell the other, the answer was no. Whether one believes or not, I found the idea intriguing. I got the bright idea that I'd like a prayer rod. Ironically, I made it a matter of prayer.

I didn't have my notebook in front of me that night; it was in the desk drawer near where I was kneeling. "Rise up," I was told, "and write the things which I shall speak."

That's how answers come to me sometimes. I get feelings, impressions, and ideas, but sometimes I get sentences. It's been that way since I was a child. About the time I left for the mission field, I approached a trusted mentor who was several years older and blessed with more experience. Without offering any context, I asked, "Does God ever speak to you in sentences?"

She answered definitively and without hesitation: "Don't ever doubt that." That's all she said. Her tone and expression conveyed some deep understanding I only came to appreciate much later.

You may debate whether it was God speaking to me, or some departed loved one, or some unspecified agent of the Universe, or my imagination. Whatever your answer, my tried-and-true practice has been to honor my mentor's advice. I've been disappointed and discouraged when I've doubted. When I've trusted and gone forward, I've found success and clarity.

The night I asked about those prayer rods, my answer came in sentences. I got up, as instructed, and sat at my desk. I pulled out my notebook and began to write. Frequently when I've received such things, the message came in language similar to the King James Version of the Bible, probably because I was so familiar with that version. I suspect the voice and the language is different for everyone according to his or her circumstances.

"I have answered thy prayers," the voice told me, "for I have granted thee a gift . . . thou hast a rod in thine hand by which thou mayest have answers to thy prayers, therefore neglect not thy gift."

I wrote as I listened, not fully appreciating the message. I was literally writing the words in my notebook when I paused and looked at the pen in my hand. It was a gold pen I'd received as a gift. I smiled as I thought back over the years of direction I'd received through that precious little rod in my hand. God is kind and has a sense of humor.

The other notebook experience came when I was researching the life of an individual who'd been dead for many years. I was part of a committee. We gathered around a conference table regularly to discuss the progress of the work. One evening I sat with a dozen committee members around the table. I sat with my back to the open door and the empty chairs along the wall.

As the committee discussed various matters, I became aware of the arrival of an unexpected guest. Though I was facing away from the door, my spiritual eyes were opened and I could see behind me. I could see in every direction. I could see every detail in my visitor's face. He was the subject of the committee's research. I'd never met him, but I knew who he was. I could feel his love. He had a pleasant, calm countenance. He entered the room behind me and sat in one of the chairs near the door.

I looked around the table. People continued their conversations. I was the only person aware of his presence. He stood and walked to a position directly behind me. He placed his hands on my head. In addition to feeling the weight of his hands, I felt a thrill surge through my being, electrifying every cell. I fought to hold back tears. I feared it might all end if someone noticed my emotions and asked me a question.

He began to speak, giving counsel and encouragement. No one else heard him, and I don't know why he came to me. I was in no position of responsibility on the committee. I was just a member, like the rest. I contemplated each word he said and tried to commit them to memory. He stopped. He discerned my disappointment and promised he'd return to give me the rest of his message. Then he left. The rest of the meeting was uneventful. I struggled to remain engaged. I wanted to go look in the hallway to see if my benefactor might be lingering. I knew better, but the thought still crossed my mind.

I continued my research at home. A few days later, I sat at a table in my living room, stacks of books and papers spread out in front of me. My visitor returned, as promised, and in almost the same manner. He appeared behind me. I saw him as before. He rested his hands on my head and began to bless me, repeating the words he'd spoken days earlier. Then he stopped as he had before. I felt disappointed. I thought I might have done something wrong to cause him to stop. I asked if I could write down the things he'd said. He responded that I could and explained that the reason he'd paused was to allow me to write. When my notes captured what he'd said, he resumed speaking, and I continued writing. He gave me explicit and detailed directions about my assignment. Steeped in experience, he instructed me to hold his counsel in confidence until the committee had completed its work, lest anyone's agency be abridged or contributions inhibited. Those instructions served me well. I still have my verbatim record of the communication.

I'm not sure I'd have received either of these profound experiences if I'd not been prepared to write them down. I do know that many times I've been richly blessed by the principles of the notebook. I've shared these principles with others, and their lives have been similarly enriched. Not all experiences are for writing, however. I've occasionally been expressly instructed to not write. Writing must be individualized to the time and circumstance.

Jeff and I have both used notebooks, though we learned the principles independent of one another and before we met. My understanding evolved from my junior high experience. I've never asked how he came to the same practice. Though we both served as Christian missionaries—he in Scotland, me in England—using a notebook for prayer was never part of our training.

That I served a mission shouldn't suggest intolerance of any other religion. I have genuine heartfelt respect for virtually all religious beliefs, even those I may not agree with. I've studied the Qur'an and the Bhagavad Gita, in part, to better understand my Muslim and Hindu friends, more particularly to better understand the billions of people who embrace those traditions. I've studied the Torah in depth, much of it in Hebrew. I have Jewish blood, and one of my ancestors studied to become a Rabbi. I love the traditions of the Jews, and I observe some of their ancient holy days. I learned Hebrew to better understand the Torah. I tried learning Greek to better understand the New Testament, but I didn't get very far with that language. To a lesser extent, I've studied Buddhism and the religious beliefs of various Native American tribes. I've read the Old Testament at least a dozen times and the Book of Mormon and New Testament between 30 and 50 times each. I love religions, ancient and modern, and the sacred texts and traditions they espouse. They all teach us something about ourselves. I see many more similarities across religious boundaries than differences, and I focus on those similarities.

With all that said, I wish to make it clear that I view spirituality largely independent of religion. I may refer to my Creator as God (or capitalize other titles referring to the Divine) but that is not intended to devalue any name or title used by others. I tend to use masculine pronouns, but I know there's an equal, omniscient and infinitely compassionate female presence in heaven. Culture and religion inevitably influence how we interpret experiences and the words we use to describe them, but I view NDEs, SDEs, and other similar phenomena as spiritual, not religious. Religion is a prickly thing. It brings comfort and purpose to many, but it can also be polarizing. Throughout this book, I try to use language that is inclusive and inoffensive. If anything I say about your religious beliefs is inaccurate or insensitive, it's unintentional and I apologize in advance.

Despite my attempts to be neutral, some of my experiences are inextricably intertwined with my Christian background and are best told in the New Testament context in which I received them. In some cases, if I were to extract my experiences too forcefully from their context, the lessons I learned would be distorted. When I share such accounts in words or examples that are familiar to me, I'm not trying to proselyte or to demean any religious tradition; I'm just sharing what happened to me. I may call it a voice, an impression, a prompting, or a spiritual feeling. I may say God spoke to me. Those are just the words I use to describe the ineffable. Feel free to apply different words or symbols to make my experiences work for you.

As I said, Jeff and I have a lot in common. Many of our spiritual experiences were similar—not in the circumstances, but in the feelings and lessons we learned independently. That we learned independently and then shared with one another proved a powerful reassurance to each of us. Our shared religious background allowed us to converse in common terms and concepts, though we've long agreed that most of our experiences were spiritual, not religious.

In at least one way, Jeff and I are quite different. He seems naturally inclined to compassion and service. For me it's a struggle. I know compassion is godly and service essential, but I labor to behave in accord with what I know. Years before I met Jeff, I made it a matter of study and prayer. I made every effort to live what I learned, and I petitioned heaven for help. I felt reassured and encouraged, but I was also told that I couldn't understand charity until I had children of my own.

I hasten to say that that message was for me, not anyone else. Most people can practice charity without being parents. I know that. My path was different. My nature required me to be a parent before I could get outside myself enough to care about another soul more than me, and that's embarrassing to admit. I thought I loved my wife and parents and siblings more than myself. I had friends I thought I loved more than myself. When I had children, I understood. Much later, when I had grandchildren, I understood more.

In my grandchildren, I see perfection personified, and not in a syrupy, sentimental, grandparent sort of way; I mean it literally. I see human beings incapable of doing wrong. They may break a dish or spill a drink or be ornery or temperamental, or write on the wall with a crayon, but they are merely learning. They can't actually do something wrong because they don't have the capacity in their young innocent lives to do so.

I wonder if God views us the same way: not that we can't do

wrong if we choose to, but that much of what we judge to be wrong in ourselves or others is simply learning. So much judgment comes from us, not from above. We're here to learn. That includes mistakes. Mistakes are not sins.

I listened one day as two people discussed how difficult it would be for God to sort the sinners from the righteous because of all the extenuating circumstances and the intentions of those involved. I listened quietly until asked for my opinion. It was one of those times when I knew the words came from some higher place because they taught me something as I spoke. "Maybe we'll just realize they were never sins in the first place," I said. There was a long silence.

Every scrap of human experience has value. Every shred of every encounter with every soul teaches me something. And every shred and scrap yields an opportunity to interact with others—to hinder their progress or to move them along the path home. Each interaction writes on my soul and changes me. I'm not very good at predicting who will help or how.

Late one evening in the emergency department, I entered an exam room. My patient was cold, wet, and homeless. I glanced at his feet. He had on shoes—if you could call what he wore shoes. Through the holes in his shoes, I could see the holes in his socks. I could see his feet, blistered and swollen. It wasn't yet cold enough to freeze his feet, but he had minor frostbite. The relentlessly wet stockings, and the need to walk several miles daily, had taken their toll. He was forced to walk from the shelter to the park, from the park to the shopping district, and from the shopping district back to the shelter. That was his daily trek. In my mind, I could see the path he'd worn in the snow.

My patient and I were the only two people in the room. He didn't have much to say. We both knew what needed to be done. I reached under the counter, grabbed a washbasin, and began to fill it with tepid water. Though facing away from him, I could see his distorted reflection in the chromed paper-towel dispenser. He watched pensively. As I moved toward the end of the gurney, he repositioned himself and reached for his shoelaces. He grimaced in pain as he leaned forward. I could tell it was an effort for him.

I took over the task as he lay back on the pillow with a look of appreciation.

I removed his tattered shoes and the remaining threads of his stockings. I found no evidence of infection or serious thermal injury—some blisters, some swelling, some maceration, but nothing serious. As I lowered his feet into the water, I squirted some soap on a washcloth. I looked up occasionally as I gently washed layers of the city from his feet. His hair was long, his beard unkempt, his clothing disheveled.

I could have delegated the task of washing this man's feet to others, but I was richly blessed by my small act of service. As I washed his feet, the heavens opened. In other words, the veil was drawn back. In this man who had neither possessions nor the esteem of the world, I saw the glorious and indescribable nobility of every soul who suffers. I saw that portion of him that was divine. I saw god.

Edwin McNeill Poteat caught the essence of empathy in a few short lines:

> He cannot heal who has not suffered much,
> For only sorrow, sorrow understands:
> They will not come for healing at our touch
> Who have not seen the scars upon our hands.[2]

I had a tiny taste of empathy that night as I walked through the snowy hospital parking lot in my stockings and drove home with cold wet feet. The homeless man who had given me so much left in my shoes. I'd given so little. I had a heater in my car and a dozen pairs of shoes at home. I had a home to go to. That evening I'd washed a man's feet. That night I wept.

Small and simple acts and experiences gradually changed me and how I perceived those around me. Service helps. It makes me want to be a better person. I learned much about service and empathy from a woman named Rebekah.

---

[2] "Stigmata," Edwin McNeill Poteat, 1892 – 1955.

8

REBEKAH

Rebekah entered my life in mid-1993, eight weeks after her husband's fatal car crash, four years before I met Jeff. She approached cautiously in a public space and asked where we'd met. I didn't recognize her. She was a beautiful, petite, blonde woman about my age. I thought if I'd met her before, I would have remembered. She ultimately remembered me from a previous ER encounter, one not related to her late husband's crash. He'd come to my ER, but I wasn't on duty that day.

Rebekah's youngest daughter was born just weeks before the crash. My youngest daughter was the same age and I felt an instant connection. When our paths crossed again two months later, I felt a powerful desire to help my new friend, a grieving mother of six, but I didn't know how. I wanted to carry a portion of her spiritual burden. I didn't know it then, but helping her would eventually help me. Without her, I would never have been prepared to meet Jeff.

Over the next several months I thought of Rebekah often and ran into her occasionally. We both had Friday night commitments that put us in the same location. Our conversations became increasingly frequent and heartfelt, sometimes spiritual. I privately wondered if my desire to help might be an opportunity to develop the compassion I so lacked and had admired in others.

"Follow your feelings," my wife encouraged. Sheila had been my confidant and encourager-in-chief since we married in 1986. She'd been my example in both service and insight. Often, when I'd pondered a topic at great length and come to some revolutionary understanding, I'd share it with Sheila. More than once she'd responded, "Oh, yeah, that's how I've always felt about it." She innately understood spiritual principles, and I trusted her advice.

Sometime during that winter, I heard a voice as clear and distinct as the anchor on the evening news. It came during one of my middle-of-the-night drives home from the ER. My route passed near Rebekah's home. I couldn't help but think of her. It was a quiet, snowy night, and I was tired and looking forward to bed.

"Is Rebekah's family less important in my eyes than yours?" the voice asked.

No, of course not, I thought, without delving into the question of who was asking.

"Then why should they be in yours?"

The questions were precise and accompanied by a flow of pure understanding. I immediately began to rationalize that my responsibility to my wife and children superseded all others. In the flash of selfless insight that accompanied the questions, however, I understood that the voice that spoke to my spirit loved all souls equally, and that I could (and should) do the same. I understood I could care for others without compromising the care to my own. More particularly, I understood that they were *all* my own.

With that realization came another question, a preemptive paraphrase of something I immediately recognized: "Who is your neighbor?" It was so familiar I knew the context instantly. My tutor had chosen a text I was sure to understand. I'd read it at least a hundred times.

When a taunting lawyer asked what he must do to be saved, Christ forced him to answer his own question by referring him to the law he claimed to love. The man answered, "Thou shalt love the Lord thy God . . . and thy neighbor as thyself." The lawyer immediately tried to justify himself, asking, "And who is my neighbor?" I could hear the dialogue in my head. Christ's response to the lawyer's question was the parable of the Good Samaritan.

Suddenly my circle of responsibility for the welfare of others was extended from my family and loved ones to my acquaintances, to strangers, even enemies, and to my worldwide circle of neighbors. They were all my family, and, at that moment, I felt an unbounded love for them all equally. I knew I had to do something.

I spent time on my knees, first asking what I should pray for, then following the directions I received. I felt prompted to ask if I might learn vicariously from the experiences of others. I understood I didn't have the capacity, time, or circumstance to learn all I needed from personal experience, but I could learn it another way. It would not be easy. In fact, I was told I would pass through my personal crucible in the process. I naïvely went forward.

Within days, I felt a strong impression to visit my mother because there were things she'd never told me about my brother's death, things she wouldn't tell me unless I asked. I soon visited her at her home—the same home where Stan and I had lived as children. My father was out of town, so we had the home to ourselves for the afternoon. She fixed lunch, and we enjoyed some pleasant conversation. Then I asked if there were things about Stan's death she'd never shared. Her expression saddened. Tears soon flowed. That was the day she told me how I'd stopped singing. I'd never heard that before. It was a powerful observation she'd kept to herself for nearly a quarter of a century. She struggled to compose herself and continued. She told me how she'd come to resent God. She'd been angry with her Maker. She admitted that it frightened her to be angry with her Heavenly Father.

My mother is the most saintly woman I've ever known, and I'd never imagined the deep feelings she described. She'd continued taking her other three children to church. She'd smiled through her anguish and loved us immeasurably through every painful day. She'd held us all together as she cracked and crumbled in places no one could see.

Before my visit that day, I'd never heard my mother speak of voices, visions or divine visitations. She is a gentle, kind woman who I'd always assumed was close to God, but I'd never heard her talk of unusual manifestations. She looked at me and again became tearful. Then she shared one of her defining moments. Home alone, cleaning the house and marching through another horrible day, three prayerless years after her firstborn's death, she asked the right question. I don't know how many times she'd asked it before, but she asked it again on that day: "How could you take my oldest son?"

She heard a voice so clear and distinct she turned around to see who was speaking. "I loved you so much, I gave my only Son."

Those few words redeemed my mother. She was able to start moving past the resentment and anger to resume her life. She was able to pray again. Her experience wrapped itself around me as she shared it, and it has never left me. I weep every time I think of it. It changed me. I didn't live it personally, but I experienced it vicariously. I walked away a different man.

Perhaps my mother's experience opened my heart to the depth of Rebekah's pain. It emboldened me or gave me enough courage to trust God. I prayed that I might take some measure of Rebekah's spiritual burden and carry it for her. I knew she had financial resources; she didn't need my money. Friends and family had helped her in many ways and as much as they could. Most of her helpers, though, had by then gone on with their lives, while Rebekah's soul-destroying darkness lingered. That, I knew, was where she needed help.

I couldn't have comprehended the depth of what I had asked for or what the response might be. I was aware of only one example. Some believe Christ took upon himself all the spiritual burdens of mankind. Contemplating what I had prayed for seemed almost blasphemous. When I spoke with a friend, he told me my request was doctrinally errant and impossible.

Despite my naïveté, or because of it, I had asked anyway. To my surprise, the answer was yes. The blackness of Rebekah's life settled onto mine and hovered there for years. It came in waves and colored every good thing I experienced. Had I known what it would feel like or how long it would last, I wouldn't have had the courage to ask.

I believe there are places God won't take us unless we ask. They are places that can teach us and elevate us to a new plane, but they are so horrific that if God took us there without our requesting it, our resentment would overpower any good that might flow from the experience. I had asked. Now I was there.

In September of 1994, I had a revealing conversation with Rebekah. She reluctantly acknowledged her resentment toward Heaven. God had taken her husband and closed the heavens, giving neither comfort nor answers. I had a context to appreciate her feelings. I'd learned it vicariously from my mother. While I didn't share my mother's experience with Rebekah, it helped me empathize. I also didn't tell her about my fledgling attempt to ease her pain. I don't know whether Rebekah's burden ever felt lighter as a consequence of my actions, but the experience was soul-stretching for me.

Something must have inspired my comments that day, because the conversation moved toward something nobler than myself. Her husband's birthday had recently passed; the wounds were fresh again. I would never have suggested what I did had it not been placed in my heart as a way to help her heal. I told her she could willingly give her husband back to God. She could choose to let him go. Don had died more than a year earlier, ripped from her arms without her having a say in the matter, but, even a year after the fact, in some divine chronology that escapes a mortal explanation, she could willingly choose to return him to God. It could be her choice.

I don't know where the concept came from. It just came out of my mouth. We didn't resolve the issue that day, but we planted a seed.

The darkness waxed and waned in my life but never disappeared. It wasn't just darkness; it was a heaviness—a lonely, empty hopelessness. It was palpable. The blackness marred the past with distortion. It destroyed the present with anguish and despair. It laid waste to the future when it consumed hope.

I later learned that my worst days coincided with Rebekah's. Even my wife noticed. On one occasion, when Sheila spoke about Don's accident, I became physically ill. Suddenly I was at the scene of the crash viewing the events immediately after impact. I felt Don's emotional anguish. It outstripped his physical pain. I understood the love he felt for Rebekah, the love she fully reciprocated, and I comprehended the magnitude of their relationship and the scope of the tragedy. I don't know how I saw or felt it, either in time or in geography, but I did. I was there.

Over time, the blackness repeatedly drove me to my knees. On one occasion I reflexively pled for relief. I uttered the words I would later hear from my own son, "Please, Dad, don't hurt me anymore." In retrospect, my prayer seems like a selfish attempt to renege on a deal. After all, Rebekah's husband hadn't come back to life; she didn't have a way out. When I'd asked to help, I hadn't asked for half an experience. I was just getting started. In response to my pleas, a firm but compassionate voice said, "Not yet." I wept that night. I wondered how I could endure it another day, but what choice did I have?

My journey into Rebekah's agony was unrelenting—perhaps because hers was unrelenting. It became part of my life. One year after asking to shoulder her burden, I received a whole new level of experience. I was going about my usual activities in my home when I became suddenly and horribly ill. The heavy, sickening blackness—worse than I'd ever felt—gripped me so forcefully I had to sit down to keep from falling. Foreboding filled the room and pressed upon me from every direction. I felt hopeless and desperate. I wanted to die; I thought I might. I had no idea what was happening or why.

At the extremity of the moment, the voice that sometimes speaks to my heart said, "This is what Rebekah felt when her husband died." It was profoundly personal. I wasn't experiencing how *it* felt, detached from the love and the relationship; I was given to know how *Rebekah* felt. Individually. Personally. I wept for her.

She'd told me about that horrible day, about how she'd found a room in the hospital where she'd poured out her soul in prayer, about when the doctor told her of Don's death. She'd told me, but I hadn't understood. Now, in some small way, I did. I hadn't had her circumstances, but I'd had a portion of her feelings. I understood how critical it was to never judge someone else's experience. We see only the circumstances, and that incompletely. We may have no understanding of their feelings or their capacity to endure. A piercing, horrible experience gave me a tiny measure of empathy and a glimpse of what it meant to bear another's burden.

Those insights didn't end my experience. The weeks, then months, rolled on. Some days the loneliness was so bad I refused to talk or write about it. I couldn't bear the thought of recording it. On one occasion, I held my youngest daughter and felt an immense love for her as she fell asleep in my arms, but even the sweetness of that experience was tainted by the constant angst of some profound loss. Part of the pain centered on feeling so alone. I felt most alone in the presence of others. No one knew except my wife, and she only in part. I had a wonderful family, a comfortable house, a good job, and my health. There was no reason for me to feel the way I did, except for the personal gauntlet that had come at my own request. In most cases, when someone suffers a significant loss, people rally to help. I was made to understand that part of my trial would be that no one else would know. Loneliness was part of Rebekah's experience, and therefore part of mine. It was part of the empathy I had sought.

When I fasted and asked what I yet needed to learn, I was told that more time needed to pass. Part of the experience was to endure it longer. When I cried out, "Why does it have to be so painful?" I heard Rebekah's words echoing in my mind. Until I heard myself say it, I'd forgotten she'd asked me the exact same question. Sometimes I would get out of bed in the middle of a sleepless night to sit in a chair in my den and weep in the darkness. I was so frustrated and angry with God for taking me to such a horrible place and for keeping me there. I wondered if I'd done something wrong to deserve what I was experiencing. On my birthday I wrote in my journal, "I wonder if God is disappointed with me."

My patient wife once told me: "There's no way around some experiences; the only way to get to the other side is to go through them." That's where I was.

I eventually visited my most trusted friend and mentor. He was 35 years my senior and steeped in soul-structuring experience. He'd survived a foxhole on Okinawa and knew what it meant to commune with Eternity. I loved him—and trusted him. He leaned back in his chair, interlaced his fingers behind his head, and rested his shoes on his desk. "Empathy is a good thing," he said. That was his five-word lesson for the day. He was a master of words, and his meaning was unmistakable. He's gone now. I miss him deeply, and I'm grateful for his friendship and wisdom. Oh how I miss him!

Lacking the humility needed to learn my lesson, and now more than a year in the darkness, I again petitioned Heaven relief. This time the answer was a kind reproof mixed with encouragement. I could end the experience. I saw the path. In some spiritual realm I saw light through and beyond the darkness as I received an understanding of what I needed to do to find relief. I knew exactly how to walk into the light. I so wanted to do so. Then came the message: "If you want the greater blessing, endure it for now."

It was a painful but powerful lesson in trust. I'd been given a choice and a promise. Beyond my comprehension or wisdom was a higher power that knew me better than I knew myself, that loved me more than I loved myself, and that had a grander and nobler plan than I had comprehended. Just as Rebekah could willingly let Don go, I could make a choice. I could willingly take the more difficult path. I wasn't sure what the promised blessing would be, but I felt confident in the source of the promise. The Good Samaritan didn't pay for just one night at the inn; he promised to return and pay any cost necessary to care for a broken soul. I submitted. I trusted the voice I believed was divine and made a covenant to do whatever I was directed to do for the welfare of another soul. It was my choice. I trusted a power and wisdom that far exceeded my own.

The darkness ebbed and flowed for years; it still comes occasionally. That first year was the most wrenching, but I wasn't done. Only looking back, many years later, did I see how my experience paralleled Rebekah's. Her grief didn't end simply because she wanted it to. In some ways, it's still not ended. Perhaps it never will. I understand that, not the circumstances but the feelings. And feelings are what craft our souls and make us who we are. Feelings make us one. For that reason, empathy is a good thing.

I'm grateful for what I learned in the blackness. I don't know whether I ever really helped Rebekah, but she helped me immeasurably. A little more than a year later, I would share some of what I'd learned with Jeff.

9

SHARING

I hadn't spoken with Jeff in a month. He'd called in May to thank me for coming to see him. He didn't know I hadn't wanted to come. He didn't know Rachel had dragged me there and insisted I share. He didn't know about the knowledge I'd received during my visit to his hospital room—that we would be friends and help one another in the future, that I would share many of my experiences with him. And I didn't know how things would unfold. I was just blundering forward, hoping.

Jeff and I spoke on the phone in early July. I felt a strong impression that we needed to visit in person. He was temporarily out of the hospital at that time, not well enough to go home, but well enough to stay with his brother. I went there to see him. On that first real visit, Jeff opened his heart. I don't know why, but he did. He shared so much he was surprised when I later told him what I'd written in my journal.

I believe something or someone told Jeff to trust me, whether he knew it or not. One reason he trusted me was because I trusted him. I hadn't died, but I'd encountered many of the spiritual components of his adventure. I'd experienced virtually everything described in NDEs: fragments of a life review, forgiveness and sanctification, visits with deceased loved ones, strangers from beyond the veil asking me to do something for them, discerning the thoughts of others and having them discern mine, encounters with the Divine, seeing into the past and the future, a reprioritization of mortal aspirations, and other ineffable experiences and feelings. I'd encountered all of those things, though not all at once. I hadn't told Jeff any of that, but I think he sensed it. Somehow people know when to share.

I remember walking into a hospital room way back when I was a resident. My patient was doing well. She rested comfortably in her bed. Her husband was the only other person in the room. He'd fully recovered from the risky surgery that had saved his life months earlier, when he'd been within minutes of bleeding to death. Before I could leave, he grabbed my arm and pulled me into a chair. He wouldn't let go. He told me his NDE as if I were a trusted friend. I had the feeling he felt compelled to share it with me.

This sweet loving man had lived a deeply spiritual and fully consecrated life. He was Christian and loved his Lord. While out of his body, he saw a panorama of the ministry of Christ. He witnessed the Last Supper. He heard the apostles sing a hymn, as described in the New Testament, and he saw them break and pass bread. He saw Christ suffer in Gethsemane. He shared it all in great detail, and I felt honored to listen.

I don't know why this gentle soul felt compelled to share these things with me that day. Maybe he was told to do so. He seemed thrilled and relieved to share, and I was his safe place on that day. We kept in touch until he passed a few years later. I miss him like I miss so many others.

When Jeff and I visited in his brother's home a little more than two months after the accident, he shared a very sacred experience, one I wouldn't share had he not already published it.

He experienced himself holding his deceased son, 14-month-old Griffin, and, in turn, being held by a Divine Presence, a being of incomprehensible light. Then he was given the opportunity to willingly give his son back to God. Griffin had been taken from him, but now he was given the privilege to choose.

It all rang true. I'd had the same conversation with Rebekah years earlier. In my own experience, I'd also been given the opportunity to choose. Jeff was cautious and uncertain as we began. When I received what he shared without questioning and told him how I knew it was true, he shared more.

"I'm impressed with him," I wrote of Jeff that night. "He's a very spiritual person." My journal entry was longer than usual and offered interesting details. I knew our conversation was the first of many. Further, I realized my experiences of the last few years were, in part, to enable me to empathize with Jeff. I understood his feelings. "I realized tonight . . . that I knew how to help him." Because of that, I knew it was worth the pain I'd experienced. I was finally grateful for the pain. And I understood the importance of time.

I'd lost those memories in the sands of the twenty-year hourglass. Perhaps some were too painful to keep in my consciousness, and I was surprised when I read them two decades later. I'm glad I was a safe place for Jeff. We've learned so much together over the years. Learning is a challenge and it takes time. Sharing helps, but only when it's in a safe place.

Sometimes the people we love and trust won't like what we have to say, especially if it contradicts what they believe. Some would have you change your experience—as if that were an option—rather than change their beliefs. Your safe place may not be in their comfort zone. They might not understand that what you are saying is simply what you experienced and that it contradicts what *you* believe—or, at least, what you used to believe. That's why you're sharing, to put it all together in a new paradigm.

One key to finding a safe place is to *be* a safe place. The questions I posed to Jeff during our visits would not have set well with many of my friends. Some people I know would have scoffed and rejected me even before hearing me out. The same was true for Jeff. Sometimes he'd share, then raise an eyebrow and wait for my skepticism or incredulity. Initially, he seemed surprised that I offered neither. I thought we were just friends, and I was just listening. Years later, he told me others were less accepting and thought I should be less accepting too, as if my acceptance somehow validated Jeff's outrageous experience to their detriment. I know at least one person told him he ought to stop talking to me.

I try to quash my judgments and doubts, to listen first and be patient. Many conversations between Jeff and I concluded with a promise by one or both of us to think about it more and revisit it later.

There's another key to finding a safe place, but it is not something I can really explain. It's a nebulous gestalt. More correctly, it's a spiritual feeling. I get a sense when someone is listening and when they understand. Others have said the same to me. They know; they've been there. When I sense that a person understands what I'm saying, I trust my impression and inch a bit closer. When I know, I seize the precious and infrequent opportunity. We help one another.

From a spiritual perspective, Jeff had had a near-death experience; from a former-bull-rider-ER-doc's perspective, he'd had a damn-near-dead experience, and he wasn't done. Our first real visit was cut short when a complication of his severe abdominal injuries and surgeries caused him to become abruptly and violently ill. I offered a quick good-bye as his brother took him urgently back to the hospital.

10

FRIENDS

When **I arrived** in the emergency department, I heard a familiar commotion. I turned to see a frail elderly woman unconscious on a gurney. Her medical team worked frantically to resuscitate her. She was already intubated. Paramedics took turns compressing her chest. I heard ribs breaking. I soon learned she lived—if you can call what she did living—in a nursing home. She couldn't speak or feed herself, or get out of bed. She was unable to recognize the few family members who rarely visited. Her condition offered no hope for improvement.

Because I'd just walked in, and because I wasn't involved in her care, my mind and heart were free from the demands and preoccupations of my job. Sometimes we're just too busy to hear or feel or see. As I watched I had a powerful spiritual feeling about the noble soul trapped in that failing body. I walked inconspicuously to the bedside and rested my hand on her right leg. Touch is so powerful. It breaks unseen barriers and invites a spiritual connection.

Busy professionals around the gurney continued their work. The unconscious woman communicated to me that she just wanted to leave this world with some shred of dignity. For some reason, she felt she needed my assistance.

Initially I did nothing except listen and acknowledge her eight decades of honorable life. In our shared silent communication, I expressed my feeling that she could go. If she wanted to leave and felt it was the right time, she could go. All I did was silently offer an unconscious woman my thoughts. I didn't do anything with regards to her medical care. There was nothing for me to do. Everyone else was doing it. I just listened and silently shared the feelings that came to me from some eternal place.

Everyone else in the room continued their activities uninterrupted. I stepped back from the gurney as her last signs of cardiac activity ceased. She left her mortal body and lingered for a moment. I saw her standing above the floor, an attractive woman who appeared to be about half the age of her now-lifeless body. She looked down on the commotion with a profound sense of peace. Her peacefulness settled over me and took me for a moment to a more glorious place. She calmly, almost casually, turned to leave. Before departing, she thanked me for answering her last earthly request. I don't know why she needed my help, but she asked. No one else in the room knew what had happened. Spirits are so grateful for our help.

As I'd struggled from the darkness, still more than a year before meeting Jeff, I'd made my covenant to forget myself and serve others. Sometimes that meant helping souls who were already on the other side of the veil, like this elderly woman in the ER. More often it meant helping the person next to me. I had so much to learn and so much to do. Several gifted people came in short succession to help me.

In March of 1996, I met Susan. I don't recall how our conversation started, but she impressed me immediately. I just had a feeling—that gestalt I mentioned earlier. She and her three young sons were visiting from out of town. Her husband had recently died from cancer, and she was considering a move to Utah. My heart told me to do something.

Two days later, Susan met Sheila in our home. In the midst of an innocuous conversation, I saw her soul. I looked on a spirit— her spirit—in a way I'd never experienced previously. I saw all that was good and bright and happy, all that was love. In that moment, her soul was delivered from the grief of her recent loss. I saw her without the sorrow. I came to realize we'd already known each other for an eternity.

I don't know how or why these things happen. I'm deeply grateful for such experiences, but I can't explain them. Sheila and I opened our home to Susan and her sons so she could move to Utah and start her new life. In return, she gave me friendship. She taught me something about breathing and feeling the presence of unseen souls.

One medical term for taking in breath is to *inspire.* Drawing in air in a conscious intentional way can invite us to feel more, to hear and see more. It can literally inspire us. Susan taught me that. Later, she would teach me how spirits look on a person's heart as easily as mortals look on a person's hair color. I'd looked on her heart soon after we met, but she later helped me understand what I'd already experienced. When I shared spiritual insights, she treated them with great reverence as if they were precious and rare. She taught me that I could hold such experiences sacred and still speak about them if I did so at the right times and with the right people. Though I was learning from her, on one occasion she thanked me and said, "I needed to hear those things." Spiritual learning is almost always a two-way street.

Several months after meeting Susan, I went alone to the grave of her husband. I was allowed to experience the sorrow and loneliness she'd felt at his passing. In contrast to my earlier experience with Rebekah, however, I was also allowed to feel the profound comfort extended to Susan when her husband died. It had come to her from a divine place when she most needed it. Now it was coming to me. It was glorious and painful and horrible and edifying, all at the same time. It was more than I could have experienced unaided.

If I taught Susan anything, she taught me more. Then she moved away. We still communicate but seldom see each other. She was one of a small handful of people I would come to know who would listen and understand, and each of them would teach me so much.

Just days before I met Susan, I'd seen Kate in the emergency department. I'd known Kate for some time. She came regularly to the ER to do tests on patients. She faced away from me, wheeling her heavy machine into a patient's room to do the scan I'd ordered. I was concerned about her because she'd recently told me her husband was physically abusive. I called her name as I approached. When she turned her tiny frame, I saw her freshly blackened and swollen eye.

I felt a sudden void in the center of my soul as if a portion of my being had been forcefully extracted. I felt sick to my stomach. When our eyes met, I saw her heart. I knew she felt it too. I fought back tears. She struggled to swallow as her lower lip began to quiver. We looked away at the same instant, not wanting to cause a scene in the patient-care area. She went on with her scan; I went back to my patients.

I caught up to Kate a little later in a less public area. She was a selfless woman, taking in children who had been abused and abandoned by drug-addicted mothers. She loved them and healed them. I invited her to contact me when the time was right and promised I'd help. When she called, I invited her to come visit. Sheila and I opened our doors to her and her children. We offered her a safe place for as long as she needed it. Ultimately, she took a different path, but we remained close friends. Sadly, that was not the last black eye she wore to the ER. I wanted to help, but there was nothing more I could do. I was so grateful for my wife's unselfish offer. She didn't need my wrenching experiences to drive her to compassion. Sheila's always had it. It's part of her.

One month after Kate's black eye, and less than a month after I'd met Susan, tragedy struck another friend. A car struck Kathy's teenage daughter while she was jogging. An experienced emergency nurse, Kathy knew all the horrors that might follow.

And they did. I learned about the accident the next day and visited the hospital more than once. Several weeks into the ordeal, at the bedside of her unconscious daughter, I began to ask Kathy questions. She'd had spiritual experiences; I could tell. I asked about her feelings, and she shared what I expected. I asked about her uncertainty and indecision, and she acknowledged it. I asked about frustration, anger, and resentment. We weren't merely probing the stages of grief; we went much deeper. I warned her of feelings to come and offered suggestions to keep her discouragement in check. Finally, she looked into my soul and said, "How do you know these things?"

Kathy and I were able to connect because I'd been where she was spiritually. I hadn't had a child struck by a car and then left to teeter for weeks at the edge of death, but I'd had the spiritual rending those circumstances brought to Kathy. Our circumstances were very different, but our feelings were the same. I shared a fragment of the experience I'd had with Rebekah. When Kathy heard what I was saying and found comfort in it, she helped me realize the darkness in my life had had purpose and that I could use what I'd learned to help others.

Months rolled by, and Kathy and I spoke often. Her daughter improved dramatically. When I spoke with Kathy a year after the accident, she referred to me as her therapist and wanted to have lunch. Over a meal, she quietly told me as the tears streamed down her face how she was helping a friend. She'd petitioned Heaven and asked if she might bear some of her friend's spiritual burden through a painful and difficult time. The answer had been yes. She'd felt the burden settle on her spiritual shoulders. She was willingly doing that for her friend.

I mentioned to Kathy the importance of trusting in a higher and infinitely benevolent power to guide our steps. I suggested we must trust that our challenging experiences come to teach us something and to make us better than we were. She hoisted her eyebrows and showed me the palms of her hands, like she was stopping traffic. "That's it," she exclaimed. "You said what I needed to hear. You always say what I need to hear." Then she told me of a recent experience, when she heard what she described as "the most peaceful voice one could imagine." It said, "You must trust in me."

As we drove back to the hospital after lunch, I counted myself blessed for the experience. I felt so grateful. I couldn't believe so many people had come to teach me. As I pondered, Kathy began to speak. She told me I was the only person she could talk to about these things, that I was the only person who would listen and believe. She taught me the importance of sharing and believing.

Between the stresses of work and the spiritually demanding days, I tried to find respite. One thing I liked to do was test-drive exotic cars: Ferraris, Lamborghinis, high-end Porsches, and a Mercedes SL-65 to name a few. If you're a doctor, dealers assume you have resources to buy. (Most doctors, including me, don't.) When I drove the Lamborghini, the dealer called my insurance broker to make sure they would cover me if I wrecked. My insurance guy knew me well. He laughed and reassured the dealer. Then we went for a drive. It wasn't as much fun as riding a bull, but it lasted longer.

One day I pulled into a dealership and started pacing around an Acura NSX. The salesman walked up and tossed me the keys. I hadn't encountered that level of enthusiasm before. He didn't ask for my name, my driver's license, or my insurance card. He didn't ask about my intentions or my occupation. He just walked toward the passenger door and waited for me to get in. I accommodated.

As we started up the road, Julian began asking theological questions. I thought it was odd, but I wanted to drive the car and I loved to talk theology—all kinds of theology—so I answered. He began asking scriptural questions. At that time in my life I could quote chapter, verse, and text, totaling about 350 pages of scripture. I could quote a dozen references on nearly any topic. And I could argue either side of most doctrinal questions. Even while driving the car to its limits, I was enjoying the conversation more than the ride.

I'd never met Julian, but he'd heard me speak to a large gathering. He'd wanted to talk to me ever since. When he saw me on the lot, he devised a plan. He told me I could drive any car I wished as long as he could ride along and ask me his questions. It seemed like a win-win to me. I agreed as I grabbed another gear.

Like I said, I liked cars and theology. I had room for both. Later that day, after a long fast ride with Julian, I commenced a fast and observed Yom Kippur with my Jewish friends.

I'd met Julian in September of 1996. Less than a month later, he invited me to speak in a church meeting at the state prison. I was less than enthused. I'd just cared for a paroled inmate in the ER, a man who had walked out of prison and promptly back to his drug habit. He'd injected something, probably cocaine or methamphetamine, or both. Then he'd taken police on a foot chase. He arrived in handcuffs, sweating profusely and out of breath. He died soon after reaching the ER.

Despite my reservations, I accepted Julian's invitation to the prison. As I gathered my thoughts over a period of days, I received a strong and persistent impression. I'd thought repentance might be an appropriate topic for a congregation of convicted felons. Some spiritual presence told me instead to talk about forgiveness. The promptings were unmistakable and persistent. Perhaps my feelings were a reflection of the Lord's Prayer. Christ taught his followers to pray by offering them an example. His prayer did not mention repentance. It spoke of forgiveness. And beyond a plea to be forgiven, it spoke of an obligation to forgive.

The church meeting at the prison commenced with an announcement that a former congregant who had recently been paroled had now died. Specifics weren't provided, but they said enough for me to know I was about to address the friends of my recent ER patient. Suddenly he was much more human, not just an ex-con high on meth running from police and then dying. I thought about my message on forgiveness and hoped God and his recently-returned son could forgive me for my judgments.

I delivered my message. It seemed well received. For me, the meeting proved both pleasant and edifying. If speaking to incarcerated souls was an act of service, it was rewarded like other such acts—with a blessing that far exceeded the gift. Perhaps

God had forgiven me already. In the car, a compassionate voice whispered, "I was in prison and ye visited me."

The experience melted my soul and drew tears. I'd been sent to see the Divine in a place where people seldom looked. Despite all my previous experiences, and all I knew intellectually, I'd failed to see. Until I heard that kind voice, I'd been oblivious to the opportunity I had encountered. There is something much more divine in all of us than we generally appreciate. When we serve our fellow beings, we serve God. Though I often fail, I try to remember.

Like so many of my tutors, Julian moved away soon after our trip to the prison. We've kept in touch. When I recently thanked him for blessing my life, he said, "You helped me more than you know." I was surprised because I hadn't felt I'd done anything significant for him. He sent me a text: "You provided a spiritual launch pad that carried me through the next decade of my life. You helped open my eyes to things I had never before considered." I guess we both enjoyed those car rides and the blessing that flowed out of them.

Susan, Kate, Kathy, and Julian were just a few of the friends sent to teach me in that year before I met Jeff. When I reviewed my journal, I was surprised how many people had come in such a short time to accelerate my course of study. Sad to say, none of them helped my attachment disorder. They came and went. When they went, it reinforced my tendency to remain aloof from emotional attachments. Intellectually, I recognized the problems with my approach to relationships. Emotionally, it was hard to overcome.

Just four days before meeting Jeff, I spoke from a pulpit to a large group of people. In the audience were the parents of a young mother whose daughter had recently been struck by a car and killed. I knew the mother. I felt empathy for her. I spoke with her in mind. I wrote that evening about the spiritual experience I'd enjoyed while speaking and how the words that came out of my mouth were better than anything I could have conceived.

Shortly after that talk, I received a card from the mother's parents: "It seems odd to thank someone for living through painful trials but we feel that the trials you've been through have given you wisdom to help others—more than you could ever know." I was grateful for the pain that had taught me so much.

Empathy comes hard. I overheard a conversation once when a friend was called to an ecclesiastical responsibility. He was given a recommendation for an assistant, a man whom he'd never met but with whom he would be obliged to work closely. He asked about the man's character and history. I listened as a colleague described the man's struggle with addiction, his run-ins with the law, and the toll his struggle had taken on his family and his professional life. He'd hit the proverbial rock bottom and was still struggling up the other side. My friend listened patiently and carefully, and then accepted the recommendation for his soon-to-be assistant. "I love a man who has suffered much," he said. I still don't know what my friend suffered to gain the empathy that allowed him to say such a thing, but I think often about the wisdom of his statement.

Jeff Olsen has empathy. It was hard-earned, but it rests easily upon him. It's evident when he speaks. It's obvious in the way people receive his messages. Suffering can make us bitter, or it can bring us empathy. In Jeff's case, it was the latter.

11

JOURNEY

I called Jeff on July 16, 1997, fourteen weeks after his accident. It was his tenth wedding anniversary. I was concerned. Anyone who has lost a loved one knows how hard Christmases, birthdays, and anniversaries can be, especially that first year when you don't know what to expect. Mother's Day, Father's Day, the anniversary of a death—they can all creep up on the recently bereaved and take them to an ugly place.

Jeff didn't say much over the phone. His hopes for a reassuring experience on that day had not met with his expectations. I had no answers. It was one of those awkward conversations where neither party knows what to say. We didn't talk long. He called me back ten days later to invite me to dinner at his home.

Jeff's home was a safe place. I say that in the broader context of he was a safe person and it was the right (safe) time. It hadn't been right when I'd visited him in the hospital. There hadn't been time when I'd visited him at the home of his younger brother. In Jeff's home, on that day, it was right. I opened up and shared. Jeff's mother fixed us a lovely meal and then disappeared. We talked for four hours. It may have been on that day that I shared one of my sacred experiences with him, one that fit with his journey and what he'd seen while unconscious.

I'd sat alone one bright spring day in a quiet room in my home. My father came to visit me. He entered through the wall and stood in the air, his head and shoulders extending above the ceiling that was no longer there. I was wide-awake and in good health. My father was alive (he still is) and at his home, miles away, in another county. Nevertheless, he came to see me, in a closed room, in the light of day, and he spoke to me. He was calm, deliberate, and succinct. As he spoke, I enjoyed a pure influx of knowledge and understanding that far surpassed the words.

He handed me a soft leather satchel. I held it in my hands until the conclusion of our visit; then it was gone. As he spoke, he described the contents. Without opening it, I could see inside to confirm what he said.

My father said he had a gift for me and he bid me to meet him in the land of our ancestors, where I would receive the gift. In the satchel, as he explained, was everything I needed to make the journey: a passport, to identify myself to appropriate people; tokens for toll roads, bridges, and tunnels; tickets for various forms of transportation; and a map to show me the path. There was no money. He cautioned me to protect the items. If I lost them, he warned, I would not be able to buy them with money, and I wouldn't be able to make the journey without them. Finally, he made it clear that the gift he had for me was not the satchel or its contents, but what awaited me at the end of my journey.

Like most near-the-veil experiences, the brevity and simplicity of that day belied the significance or impact. I knew in an instant the grand scope of the metaphor—that my Father was inviting me to return to him, providing everything necessary for me to succeed and offering me everything he had if I would just come home.

I see Heaven's greatest gift as the profound endowment of life, a life that commenced before mortality and continues beyond death. I see others pass through mortality and read accounts of their journeys, both ancient and modern. Some accounts are chronicled in records deemed sacred or scripture. They give an example or pattern, a map and key bits of knowledge, but I still must take my own journey. Reading about, seeing, or even experiencing *their* journey doesn't take *me* home.

I fear some people mistake the instructions for the gift. They see someone else walking back into the presence of God and think they've made the journey themselves. It's akin to walking hungrily into a fully stocked kitchen, taking out a recipe for cookies, and sitting down and thinking you've been fed when you've made no effort to bake the cookies or to eat them. I believe the journey through mortality is itself a gift, but the grand endowment from Heaven is the eternal life we sometimes struggle to see, even while we're living it.

From my conversations and spiritual encounters with various souls in a broad spectrum of circumstances, I believe human beings, almost universally, long to be in places of comfort and safety. The simplest manifestation of our innate longing might be placated in our earthly home, with loved ones, or in the beauty of nature and solitude. In a larger, more spiritual sense, our longings drive us to sacred places and to our spiritual home.

Sometimes the geography of sacred places is far-reaching. Of the nearly two billion Muslims, every able-bodied soul who can afford to do so is expected to participate in the Hajj. Pilgrims are sanctified and don clean vestments before marching seven times around the Kaaba. From around the world they make the pilgrimage to Mecca to be in a sacred place. It's a symbolic journey home.

Mormons—or members of The Church of Jesus Christ of Latter-day Saints, as they prefer to be called—journey from various parts of the world, sometimes at great sacrifice and expense, to receive sacred blessings in their temples.

People of many races and religions seek to be in sacred places.

Irreligious people often meditate, arguably for the same reasons—to rejuvenate the soul and to be nearer to something more glorious than the ordinary.

Yom Kippur—the Day of Atonement—finds Jews in their synagogues, remembering ancient rites of sanctification. Christians find new birth through baptism. Some Native Americans find it through the womb of the sweat lodge. Buddhists seek a state of enlightenment in which they need not continue their otherwise endless repetition of birth. Initiation into Buddhism may include a permanent physical mark on one's body and, like many other belief systems, the taking of a new name.

When Jeff spoke to me of leaving his body, he also spoke of reentering it. Entering a body is a sacred, sometimes painful process. Most people don't recall entering their body at birth, but many recipients of NDEs recall the process vividly. When Jeff and I discussed it, I offered an Old Testament context.

The first temple in ancient Israel was a portable tent or tabernacle. The Lord instructed Moses to bring Aaron and his sons to the door of the tabernacle, to wash them, anoint them, sanctify them, and dress them in holy garments, all in order to enter the temple. This was particularly significant because Israelites, and later Christians, believed their bodies were temples. In other words, they were learning the process of entering their bodies—their mortal tabernacles, their temples. They were learning the process of birth.

In the ancient temple, a veil separated the symbolic throne of God in the Holy of Holies from other less sacred areas. The high priest passed through the veil on Yom Kippur to offer atonement for the people. Later, according to Christian tradition, the Messiah offered the Infinite Atonement, opening a new path that Christ "consecrated for us, through the veil, that is to say, his flesh" (Hebrews 10:20, KJV).

Did you catch that? According to the Apostle Paul, *Christ's veil was his flesh*. Perhaps Paul was the inspiration for Charles Wesley's 1739 lyrics to what would later be known as "Hark! The Herald Angels Sing." They spoke of Christ coming to earth "veiled in flesh." No wonder the veil in the temple was rent at the time of

Christ's death. His flesh was being rent and separated from his spirit. So, too, our flesh is our veil. It is our tabernacle or temple. The special vestments in which Aaron and his sons were clothed to enter the tabernacle anciently represented the mortal flesh with which we were clothed at birth. If you embrace the tradition of Adam and Eve, I suggest the coats of skins with which they were clothed when they left God's presence to enter this world represented exactly the same thing with which we were clothed when we did the same. They, and we, were clothed with mortality.

Near-life experiences cluster around birth and death because spirits are moving in and out of their bodies (veils), and some of that glory spills into our world before the veil slams shut. Further, we picked up a portion of the veil as we passed through it at birth. It enveloped us and caused us to forget our divine heritage.

I don't have detailed notes of my visit with Jeff that first day in his home, but I believe we talked about all of these principles in the context of him having left his body to experience the other side of the veil and to see clearly the pathway home, to gain knowledge and insight before reentering his mortal tabernacle.

Whatever we spoke about, we concluded when Jeff asked me to offer a special prayer. He sat in a chair. I stood behind him and placed my hands on his head. As I prayed on Jeff's behalf, a spiritual sanctification flowed through us. He was told that his sins were forgiven. The room was filled with the pureness of the message. It was a renewal and confirmation of what he'd experienced while out of his body. It came in an audible, tangible manner, as undeniable to his mortal senses as his NDE had been to his spiritual senses. It felt as if Heaven had customized the experience to accommodate his present need. We experienced it together. We both wept.

Rachel called a few days later to tell me she had spoken with Jeff and how much he'd appreciated my visit and how the things we'd discussed had helped him. Neither she nor Jeff knew how much it had helped me. I'd received the same blessing. It had enveloped and sanctified us both.

12

GODS

Jeff and I sat in a restaurant visiting across a table. He'd paged me early in August and told me he'd had a tough day. We met for lunch on August 12. He ate steak and paused when I asked him an unusual question. It was a natural follow-on from our discussion about tabernacles and veils and our journey home.

"When did you become a god?" I asked.

He later told me he wondered how I'd come up with the perfect question at the perfect time; how had I known what he'd experienced to ask that question? I didn't know it at the time, but Jeff's family would tease him about having an imaginary friend who'd always conjure up the exact conversation to answer his needs. One person joked that I was celestial at one moment, only to suggest Jeff stop talking to me at another.

About a year before I met Jeff, I spent time walking a friend through understanding an experience that had come to him. I think he knew the answer, but it didn't fit with what he believed. That's why he had struggled. Ultimately, he rejected what I'd shared. He saw the disappointment in my expression and asked why I was sad. "Because you're so certain about what you know, you're not willing to learn," I said.

In medicine there's an idiom: *When the diagnosis is made, all thinking stops.* It describes the unfortunate situation in which a doctor comes to an incorrect diagnosis then, because he or she thinks they know what's going on, fails to see all the evidence pointing in another direction, toward the correct diagnosis. In law enforcement, it called a rush to judgment. The same can happen in spiritual matters. That was the sad situation with my friend; he was so certain of what he thought he knew, he couldn't hear the truth. He couldn't learn.

Jeff was never that way. He was a willing learner. There was nothing special about me. I just asked the right questions at the right times. Sometimes Jeff and I were simply thinking on the same topic. Jeff didn't know this, but sometimes, before our visits, I'd pray to say the right things. Sometimes an essence more noble and intelligent than either of us would put the right words in my mouth and direct our conversation. Jeff hadn't written about his experiences yet. He'd barely talked about them except to me. He'd later write of the moment he'd held Griffin, saying, "I realized that not only was I being embraced by deity, but also that I myself was divine, and that we all are."[3]

It took Jeff ten years to get those words on a page. He was very cautious about how he characterized the experience and the message. It's hard to admit such things. He hadn't told me those words until after my question du jour, but it didn't surprise me when he said it. I'd pondered it at length and long ago come to the same conclusion. Remnants of who we are and where we came from peek out in cultures throughout the world. Coronation ceremonies from Great Britain to the isles of the Pacific, and many places in between, share interesting and common hints to our identity. Most include a washing, an

---

[3] *I Knew Their Hearts* (Plain Sight Publishing, Springville, Utah, 2012), 86-87.

anointing, a new name, and being clothed in sacred vestments. Some include a reenactment of the creation story and a ritualistic acting out of the conflict between good and evil. In Greek Orthodox weddings, brides and grooms are crowned queens and kings, respectively. Remnants of our true identity are everywhere.

The Qur'an and the Bhagavad Gita both speak of a premortal existence. Early Christians shared this belief until the Second Council of Constantinople declared the doctrine to be anathema. Latter-day Saints stand out among Christians for their belief in life before birth. They point at the Lord's words to Jeremiah— "Before I formed thee in the belly I knew thee; and before thou camest forth out of the womb I sanctified thee, and I ordained thee a prophet"—as evidence of pre-earth sentience and the sanctifying process of birth. They, more than most, profess they are literal spiritual offspring of God. While others interpret ancient texts and traditions less literally, a broad array of cultures and traditions affirm a portion of the Divine dwells in every soul. And, with that divine nature and pre-earth existence, comes an eternity of experience and knowledge.

My inability to remember my premortal existence or my divine origin doesn't change who I am. Human beings are not mere bundles of biological happenstance in a cosmos of coincidence. To continue the Israelite metaphor, I'm in the tabernacle of my mortal body, behind a veil, in the Holy of Holies. I just fail at times to realize it.

I asked Jeff questions for a reason. Formulating the right question is key to finding the right answer. The right question for him at that moment was, "When did you become a god?"

"I have always been a god," he said, though he'd only recently realized it. He knew the answer from his NDE; I knew it from my near-life experiences. That was the first time he'd said it out loud, and he hadn't had time to contemplate a doctrinal explanation for his first-hand experience.

Most people don't say things like that out loud. For most, such a thought is blasphemous; saying it aloud in certain circles and in times past might have been a capital offense. Some religious or cultural paradigms accept the notion of being children of god, or the idea of striving to be more like god, or even becoming gods in some future day, but they entertain such ideas in the abstract.

I shared my thoughts with Jeff in the New Testament vernacular we both knew. I reminded him of Christ's response to those who accused him of blasphemy and sought to stone him for claiming to be a son of God. "Jesus answered them, Is it not written in your law, I said, Ye are gods?" (John 10:34, KJV). Christ was talking to those who hated him enough to kill him and he was telling them they were gods. He wasn't defining some new doctrine. He wasn't teaching some soon-to-be Christian principle. He was quoting already ancient text his listeners accepted as scripture: "Ye are gods; and all of you are children of the most High" (Psalms 82:6, KJV). How could anyone state it more explicitly?

When I was born of mortal parents, I became mortal by virtue of my birth. I didn't have to do anything more to realize my mortality. I didn't have to grow to maturity or become famous or otherwise prove myself. I was mortal.

So it is with my divine parentage. By virtue of being a child of God, I am a god already. I may grow and learn and become more like my Divine Parents, but I am a god already. I say that with absolute reverence and respect. In my mind, the statement in no way denigrates or demeans God. I may labor to become more like God—kinder, more patient, more loving, and more forgiving—but that doesn't negate what I am by virtue of my divine heritage.

I think it's important to note what Christ did *not* say. Neither Christ nor the psalmist said you may *become* gods if you do everything perfect and overcome the frailties and foibles and follies of the world. If that were the case, we might come to the naïve and disastrous conclusion that we somehow earned it. No. They spoke in the present tense: you *are* gods. To see ourselves as less is to demean our spiritual parentage.

As important as it is to realize who I am, it is equally important for me to understand who my neighbors are. When I see every broken, struggling soul as a child of God and a divine sibling—gods already—I behave better and treat others better too.

Jeff and I would go on for hours. Sometimes the servers wouldn't even come back to refill our drinks, probably because they wanted us to clear out and make room for others. (Because of our long visits, we left big tips.) We would go back and forth, sharing experiences and reaffirming what we'd learned. A year earlier a dear friend had told me, "You should teach people in such a way as to cause them to feel they have always known it." That epitomized my visits with Jeff. He and I had always known it; we were just helping each other remember.

Let me borrow one more gem from the Judeo-Christian cannon to emphasize my point about who we are. When David was presented with an opportunity to kill Saul—the man that had attempted to kill him—David said, "The Lord forbid that I should do this thing unto my master, the Lord's anointed, to stretch forth mine hand against him, seeing he is the anointed of the Lord" (1 Samuel 24:6, KJV).

David was unwilling to act against the Lord's anointed king. I try to follow David's example. And, when I wonder just who the Lord's anointed are—these kings and queens—I think of those ancient Israelites who were anointed and clothed in sacred apparel in order to enter the tabernacle. Then I'm reminded that every soul on earth was anointed and clothed in the sacred veil of mortality in order to enter their tabernacle of clay at birth. Every person you see, by virtue of his or her birth, is the Lord's anointed and deserves to be treated as such.

Too often, the most difficult place to see God is in the mirror. I see the Divine in other individuals—better since my trip to the prison, and after washing the feet of my homeless tutor—but I still struggle at times to see it in myself. The veil can be thick and the fear overwhelming, but seeing who you are offers great promise and carries unmeasured responsibility.

Jeff had moved rapidly and far along his path. Our conversations were fun and uplifting and instructive. I was again impressed that day that we would have a meaningful and lasting friendship. Sharing with him helped me. I was still finding my way out of the darkness, and having such a friend made things easier. "Life is better for me than it has been in a long time," I wrote. "I feel less burdened, less tormented, less uncertain."

13

PATIENCE

Occasionally **I awake** from what I know was more than a
dream. August 1997 saw such a day. I sat up in bed with a
strange realization that I'd just witnessed something profound. I'd
seen British soldiers in early twentieth-century uniforms
slaughtering hundreds of peaceful unarmed demonstrators in
India. I had an inexplicable knowledge that my dream had
something to do with Mahatma Gandhi.

I'd heard of Gandhi but knew little about him. I knew even
less about India's struggle for independence from Britain. I
decided to learn more. I studied Gandhi's life. I read the
Bhagavad Gita to better understand what he believed. Gandhi
impressed me with his determination, his fasting, and his
commitment to non-violent resistance. Because of my love of
varied religious traditions, I particularly connected with his
statement, "I am a Muslim and a Hindu and a Christian and a Jew

and so are all of you." In another version of the quote, he included himself among the Buddhists as well. After more reading, I realized my dream had shown me the Amritsar Massacre of April 13, 1919, when a British general ordered troops to fire into an unarmed crowd, killing nearly 400 peaceful Indians. I'm not sure why I had that dream, but I think it was to help me learn something.

Long before I'd heard of Gandhi, I'd fasted and made offerings on a regular basis. That's not unique. Millions of people from various backgrounds fast and make offerings. After my dream and my studies, however, my fasting changed. I came to appreciate Gandhi's observation, "Poverty is the worst form of violence." I felt inclined to fast and make an offering specifically to benefit the poor and hungry throughout the world. In the process, I was struck by the insignificance of my offering. I could give everything I had and it would feed only a handful of people, and only for a brief period. My contribution was infinitesimally small compared to what was needed. Yet, as I thought about my small gift, a warm voice whispered, "But I can feed them all."

Suddenly I understood it was not about the magnitude of my gift; it was the act of giving. It was about having a heightened consciousness of the need and doing *something*, no matter how small. We each contribute in different ways, balanced somewhere in the innumerable intersections of opportunity, ability and personal priorities. Some offerings are visible; others, equally important, go unnoticed. All are mingled and magnified by an unseen Benevolence, making the gift larger than the giver. If a carpenter's son can feed a multitude with a few loaves and a handful of fishes, surely the Architect of the universe can magnify my tiny gift to "feed them all."

I tried to focus less on what I couldn't do and more on what I could. I could do something small. I could help the person next to me. Three weeks after my dream about Gandhi, I gained another life-changing insight. I didn't connect the two experiences at the time, but now I see them as intertwined.

On a beautiful clear day, as I looked out across fields of hay and livestock, I saw myself literally shaking the encumbrances of the world from my person, like shaking drops of rain from an overcoat. It was as if I was dusting everything temporal from my soul. As I watched, I transitioned from merely seeing myself to actually experiencing the process. And, as I experienced it, I continued observing it from nearby. I know that's not possible in the mortal world, but that's what happened.

As I shook all worldly possessions from my being, I slowly passed through an indistinct veil and walked into a beautiful lush landscape on the other side. I felt a gentle brush slide past my face and arms as I emerged into a new, brilliantly pleasant place. I felt sanctified, wearing clean, but well-worn blue jeans and a simple white shirt with a button-down collar, no shoes or socks, nothing else. I had no belt, no jewelry, no hat, and nothing in my pockets. And, I'm pleased to say, no tie. I was completely disencumbered from the things of the world and fully given over to the will of Heaven. As I walked through the field, the ground embraced my bare feet and welcomed me. I enjoyed an intensely liberating realization that I possessed nothing, missed nothing, and wanted nothing. The mania of acquiring things had fled. I understood that the things of the world had no value except to care for others. I was free.

I don't know whether to characterize what happened as a vision, a waking dream, an out-of-body experience, or some other near-the-veil adventure. Sometimes the words are charged with judgment from those who listen. When I have such an experience, I tend to use benign descriptors. (I know Jeff does the same.) Saying I had a vision lines me up with prophets and psychotics. Saying I had a dream is much less threatening. People who experience such things often minimize them, and use euphemisms to make those who listen less uncomfortable. The problem with calling my experience on that day a dream is that I was wide-awake. As I get further from the experience, or find myself in a safer audience, I'm more at ease calling it what it was. You can call it whatever makes you comfortable. What mattered was what I learned and how I felt. For me it was a near-life experience. I long for such moments.

As the other side of the veil taunted me with glimpses of

glory, Jeff was being pummeled back into mortality. We'd had dinner in his home early in August, but his return to home took time and painful experience. He paged me on August 24. He was struggling. I drove to his home. He'd been unpacking the luggage from the family's Easter trip—the trip that ended with the death of Tamara and Griffin. It was a hard day for him.

I hadn't shared my dream about Gandhi during our visit earlier in the month because I hadn't had time to ponder it or to study the historical context of what I'd seen. Now I felt differently. We talked at length about spiritual principles. I didn't record the details of our visit, but we shared much and strengthened one another.

While I was at Jeff's, Rachel paged. She too was having a difficult day. Perhaps I thought about my recent dream and what I had learned—to do small things, to help those close by. I went directly from Jeff's house to hers. She shared a lot but avoided discussing the real issue that was easily discerned. What I finally said, and what she later told me most helped her, was, "Don't give up."

I drove from Rachel's house to the ER and changed clothes in my truck. When I walked in, another doctor was doing CPR on a young woman who'd drowned in a hotel pool. I felt her spirit as I entered the room. Her presence increased in intensity as CPR was discontinued. I didn't see anything or receive any message. She just faded away. Every experience is different. Perhaps I projected what I wanted to feel onto my unseen angel, but just witnessing her presence for those few moments seemed like a reassurance that the day's activities had been both guided and accepted. Her brush past my spirit sustained me.

Later that week, I visited with Rebekah. She said she was doing, "Great!" I'd never heard her say that. And I'd never seen such happiness in her eyes. She'd finally enjoyed the spiritual experience she'd longed for and which gave her peace. It was now more than four years since her husband's death, and she'd finally found some respite. What she described was beautiful. What she felt constrained to not say seemed even more glorious. Initially I was thrilled for her, then something sinister took over.

I'm ashamed to admit it. I was jealous. I felt depressed and discouraged all evening. I'd had uplifting spiritual experiences and momentary reprieves, but the darkness still tormented me daily. Why did Rebekah get this wonderful experience? Why couldn't I find what I was looking for? If a God loved me, why wouldn't he embrace me as he'd embraced Jeff and Griffin? Why? Why? Why? I had a thousand selfish questions and as many tears. I was genuinely happy for Rebekah but filled with self-pity. I felt lonely and frustrated and hopeless. I felt embarrassed, and I was glad no one could read my thoughts.

Earlier that morning, before I'd met with Rebekah, I'd visited my mentor—the same one who'd told me that empathy was a good thing. We'd visited for an hour. We hadn't talked about the details of my struggle, but we'd touched the tops of the waves. He knew I was working through a difficult time and that I was impatient. His words came storming back that night to rescue me from wallowing in my selfishness. I heard his calm voice from earlier in the day: "Faith in the Lord includes faith in his timing."

14

BIRTH

Dave **Boone was** a sweet and kind man. He was about twenty years older than me, in his mid-50s at the time. Despite the cerebral palsy that had robbed him of the ability to walk, he seemed perpetually happy. Dave's difficulties with speech often left people with the misimpression that he was mentally disabled. He was not. He was bright and thoughtful. It took time for him to articulate a concept, but it was worth the wait. Dave's personality made me want to be a better person. He often caused me to ponder the limitations that mortal tabernacles place on divine spirits.

In early September, I visited Dave in the hospital, where he struggled to breathe through his pneumonia. I held his hand as we talked. It's amazing how much a touch can communicate—how it can connect two people, spirit to spirit. I'd known Dave for years. We were neighbors, and I'd visited him in his home many times. He looked forward to what he believed would be a glorious next phase of existence, free from the limitations he'd experienced in this plane. He'd be able to move freely and speak clearly. When I visited him in the hospital, he knew he wouldn't be going back to his house; he'd be going home instead. I told him I loved him and kissed him on the top of his nearly-bald head as I left. He died a few days later.

On the day Dave died, I spoke with Scott, an old friend who'd struggled through difficult times: divorce, professional setbacks, and substance abuse. He needed a friend. I'd felt impressed to call him several months earlier. When I had done so, he expressed suspicion. He asked why I'd reached out. I told him I thought it was time I stopped being an absentee friend. He asked whom I'd been talking to and why I was calling. I hadn't spoken to anyone; I told him so. He asked again why I'd called. I said, "Because I felt impressed to do so." I heard a deep sigh on the other end of the line and a softening in his tone. He said, "I just wanted to hear you say it."

Not long after that, Scott called me in the middle of the night. He was despondent and sobbing. He'd had a shotgun in his mouth moments before. I talked him down as best I could. He refused to come to me. He refused to give me his address to enable me to go to him. So we talked about things that mattered until the situation de-escalated. Over a number of months, things got better for him. Now, on the day of Dave's death, Scott shared his excitement about a new life and the prospect of baptism.

Later the same day, I called Jeff. As Dave was enjoying the liberation of his spirit from his imperfect body, Jeff was forced to be all too aware of his. He was struggling with his prosthetic leg. Maturing a stump takes time, especially if you're gaining or losing weight. If the stump doesn't fit into the prosthesis properly, it can lead to sores and infection, a major setback in the whole process. Fortunately, Jeff had a good prosthetist.

Dave's death and Scott's prospect of baptism both influenced my conversations with Jeff. Baptism may sound like an odd topic, but Jeff and I often discussed the similarities we saw across cultural and religious divides. When Catholics enter cathedrals, they often dip their finger in holy water and cross themselves as a renewal of their baptism. A billion Hindus find the waters of the Ganges equally sacred and sanctifying. The sweat lodge offers rebirth to certain Native Americans. These concepts are larger than religion. Birth, death, and baptism are intimately related and rife with clues about our past and future.

Birth and death are so intertwined they are usually experienced together. When we're born, we experience a form of spiritual death in that we are separated from God. The veil of our mortal tabernacle hinders the intimate contact we once enjoyed. And when we die, we are reborn into a new existence. Birth and death go together. I think of it this way: birth is a union or reunion, and death is a separation. Mortal birth is the union of body and spirit, preceded by the separation of our spirits from God. Mortal death—the separation of body and spirit—precedes the reunion of our spirits with God, which is a spiritual rebirth.

The Apostle Paul connected birth, death, baptism, and resurrection with Christ. He wrote, "we are buried with him by baptism into death: that like as Christ was raised up from the dead by the glory of the Father, even so we also should walk in newness of life. For if we have been planted together in the likeness of his death, we shall be also in the likeness of his resurrection" (Romans 6:3-5, KJV).

It seems that whatever birth we experienced in a spiritual realm was followed by a mortal birth, which may be followed by a spiritual rebirth (baptism) and a mortal rebirth (resurrection). Some people who don't like the idea of reincarnation accept the notion of being repeatedly reborn as long as one just uses different words to describe the process. Jeff and I discussed the principles at the time and circled back to the topic two years later when I came to a greater understanding.

In 1999, I had the privilege of witnessing a number of baptisms over a period of weeks. As I watched people descend into the water and come forth again, the eyes of my understanding were opened. The walls and ceiling of the baptistery faded away, and a glorious concourse of souls became visible. The group seemed innumerable. I understood they'd gathered to witness and rejoice in the ordinances being performed.

For a week I pondered the marvelous experience I'd been given. Then I returned to the same font and experienced the same vision again, and this time I inquired as to why a simple ordinance was so profound as to draw such rejoicing from a vast host of witnesses. I'd managed to formulate the right question. In that moment, I comprehended what was being represented.

I saw endless hosts of souls desiring mortality. They sought to leave their familiar circumstance, where they could hear and see and move freely, for an opportunity to be immersed into another realm—into a body that is composed largely of water—to experience impaired vision, muted hearing and a limited capacity to move and act. They desired to lay aside a portion of their glory in order to learn and grow. And they were willing to stay here, in this life, until the same benevolent Creator who'd allowed them to come raised them up again to a newness of life. Then they would again see clearly and discern perfectly between right and wrong, hear the voice of their Creator without the din of background noise, and move and act without the wearying restrictions of mortality.

I understood baptism, whether in the Jordan River, the Ganges, the sweat lodge, or in some other font, represented the whole mortal experience—birth, death, burial, resurrection, and everything that comes between. Baptism has been segmented and adapted to various cultures and traditions, but what it represents is universal. That's what I saw.

I have to admit, I envied Dave Boone's opportunity to go home. I think I envied Jeff at times, too, for what he'd been allowed to see and experience. I always fight a twinge of envy when I attend a funeral. I find myself looking beyond the casket to the rejoicing we rarely see. Whatever rejoicing we experience when a child is born, that same rejoicing is magnified beyond the veil when someone dies and is welcomed home. Birth and death are two ends of mortality, but they are only mile markers in our larger journey. I believe there is sorrow and rejoicing, excitement and anxiety—perhaps even something akin to a funeral—in the world of spirits every time a soul leaves their loved ones to embark on mortality. While we rejoice the infant's arrival, they comfort one another through the sorrow of separation. Then, it's all reversed at death.

A week after Dave's death, I cared for a woman in the ER. She didn't survive. As the fervor of the resuscitation team began to dissipate, I took in one of those slow controlled breaths I'd learned from Susan. You can miss so much if you're too busy; you can experience so much if you pause and offer yourself. When I paused and took that inspiring breath, my patient responded. Before she left, she said, "I'm okay. I'm happy. Thank you for trying. It was my time. I'm no longer in pain."

15

GO

The voice said, "Go." I was sitting in a meeting in mid-October when I heard it. Dave Boone had passed a month earlier. I'd spoken with Jeff a couple of times. He was doing well. When the voice said, "Go," I had no reason to refuse. I didn't know why, but I knew where and when, so I made plans to go. A special event had been scheduled in another city, and for some reason I needed to be there. A ticket wouldn't be easy to obtain, but that was okay. I hadn't been told to attend the event, just to go to the city.

I called a friend the next day to talk about something completely unrelated. "I have your ticket," she said, without asking why I'd called.

"What ticket?" I asked.

She had a ticket to the event and said it was for me. I told her about the message I'd received, knowing she'd understand. She wasn't surprised. She'd known since the ticket had come into her hands. She always knew. I booked a hotel room and adjusted my work schedule so I could go. I didn't know why I'd been directed to go instead of someone else, but it may have been simply because I was willing.

I visited Jeff in late October. I noted in my journal how much he'd grown, how much he'd learned. "He has a strong and sensitive countenance," I wrote. It had been seven months since the accident. I don't know what else we talked about that day, but I'm virtually certain I told him about my upcoming trip and my feelings about the importance of following a prompting. I'd soon be heading out of town for no other reason than I'd been told to go.

When people ask me how to receive direction in their lives, I remind them I have no special knowledge. I just try to point them toward the light and offer a simple suggestion that has never failed me. When you meditate, contemplate, pray, or spend time in self-reflection—or whatever other practice you are comfortable with—ask Heaven, God, the Universe, the Saints or Prophets, or your inner self this question: "What can I do today to serve someone else?"

If you're willing to ask that question and act on your answer, I promise you will experience a feeling, intuition, vision, voice, dream, or some other communication that will edify you and the person you serve. I promise that you will be blessed for doing so. I know from experience. Ask the question; act on the answer. You'll know you've communed with the Divine. Once you've done it, you'll do it again and again. And you'll grow into doing it naturally.

After a long drive and a sleepless night in a hotel bed, I woke early on the day of the event. I couldn't go back to sleep. I felt impressed to go to the venue. It was still two hours before the doors would open, but I went. It felt good to be there. I somehow knew coming early was important. I walked up to a security guard and asked where the line formed for the event. "You're it," he said. A few minutes later, a young family approached: a man, a woman, and two children. We were the beginning of the line.

I'm not much of a chatterer, but we chatted. The kids were impatient, so their father took them for a long walk. Somehow the conversation between the woman and me drifted in a serious direction. She and her husband were happy. They'd been together for some time, but there was something lacking that made her feel the family and relationship were incomplete. Her husband knew what she desired: a sacred and religious sanction of their civil marriage. He desired it too but didn't feel ready. I listened more than I spoke. The conversation drifted back to the superficial when her husband and kids returned. Soon the doors opened, and we filed in.

We sat close together, but I was soon in my own world. Music played as we waited for the event to commence. Then that voice returned. Sometimes I don't like the voice, or what it says. I'm ashamed to say that sometimes I resist or refuse. I was instructed to tell this man whom I'd barely met that it was time for him to bless himself and his wife with the solemn ceremony they both desired. I was shocked and recoiled at the thought. The message came again. It couldn't be misunderstood. I was clearly being told what I should do, but I still resisted. I was afraid.

The third time the voice spoke, it said, "This is why I brought you here. If you refuse to do this, you will be held accountable."

The rest of the event was uncomfortable. I squirmed. I contemplated the words I should say, though I didn't really need to; I'd been told exactly what to say. I struggled to trust. I wrestled with my fear. *Who was I to say such a thing?* I thought. *I don't even know these people.*

"You're the person I sent to say it," I was told. How could I argue with that?

After the event concluded, people filed from the venue. Some, including the family I'd met, lingered on the grounds. They visited on a patch of grass in the shade of a tree and greeted me warmly as I approached. Somehow the words just spilled out. The event and the conversation they were having under the tree put my words perfectly into context. I didn't need to preface the message or explain it.

"It's time," I said.

"I know," he replied.

We embraced. Tears streamed down our faces. His wife melted. She couldn't speak. They were so grateful.

I got into my car and started home. A sense of relief and gratitude overwhelmed me and moved me to tears. I'd been sent nearly 200 miles in one direction to meet a family who had traveled hundreds of miles in the other. In an empty parking lot, we'd discussed what this woman had prayed for for years. Then, on the grass, I'd said almost nothing, but it was the right thing. As I drove home, I enjoyed one of the most spiritually edifying experiences of my life. I communed with the Divine openly for hours. Heaven nurtured my spirit and made me whole.

I thought often of this young family. A few weeks later, I received news of their solemn event. A grateful wife wrote to me, "Thanks for following instructions from above." I was so grateful I'd overcome my fear.

Jeff and I spoke a lot about overcoming fear and doubt. On at least one occasion, we discussed it in the context of Peter walking on water. I have a peculiar take on what transpired with Peter and why. I've never heard anyone else explain it this way.

When Christ's disciples saw him walking toward them on the water, they feared what they thought might be a ghost. Christ identified himself and told them to not be afraid. The impetuous Peter then spoke:

> "Lord, if it's you," Peter replied, "tell me to come to you on the water."
>
> "Come," he said.
>
> Then Peter got down out of the boat, walked on the water and came toward Jesus. But when he saw the wind, he was afraid and, beginning to sink, cried out, "Lord, save me!"
>
> Immediately Jesus reached out his hand and caught him. "You of little faith," he said, "why did you doubt?" (Matthew 14:28-31, NIV)

Why did Peter sink? When I ask, people almost always say it

was because of fear or doubt. To that, I say, "Yes, but what did he doubt?" Then the answers come more slowly.

When Peter answered Christ's invitation, and stepped out of the boat, he had faith that he could walk on water. After his first steps, knowledge supplanted his faith. He knew he could walk on water. He was doing so. When the wind raged, Peter didn't doubt that he *could* walk on water; he knew by experience that he could. His fear caused him to doubt whether he *should* continue to walk on the water.

I still struggle to control the doubt and fear that keep me from doing what I should, but I'm glad I listened and responded one day in a parking lot.

16

FORGIVE

By early November, 1997, Jeff had made the decision to use his difficult and exalting experiences to help others heal. He hadn't yet decided to write his book or speak to large groups, but he'd warmed to the idea of helping people on a one-on-one basis. We'd talked about the feelings of sanctification that had accompanied his NDE and the special prayer we had shared in his home. We'd talked about how those experiences fit with the dogma of man's sinfulness and the constant need to repent. We would talk about it many times in the future. (We're still talking about it.) I recall one of those first discussions.

I met Jeff in his office. We left through the freight elevator to avoid three flights of stairs. He'd become more adept at managing his new leg, but it was still painful, especially on stairs. I've only recently come to understand how much discomfort his prosthesis and phantom pains caused. After he exited the wheel chair, his limp changed occasionally depending on his state of healing and his prosthesis. I once suggested getting a better leg and offered to help—the altruistic insurance company had again managed to come up short—but Jeff declined. We almost never talked about his medical challenges. He didn't offer; I didn't ask. We discussed other things.

Jeff seemed bugged that day. He told me about an incident in his Sunday school class. They'd discussed a New Testament account of an undisputed sinner who'd washed and anointed Christ's feet. A Pharisee named Simon asked Christ why he'd allowed the woman to do such things. He responded with a parable:

> There was a certain creditor which had two debtors: the one owed five hundred pence, and the other fifty. And when they had nothing to pay, he frankly forgave them both. Tell me therefore, which of them will love him most? Simon answered and said, I suppose that he, to whom he forgave most. And he said unto him, Thou hast rightly judged. (Luke 7:41-43, KJV)

If the creditor represented God and the debtors represented us, it's important to note that neither debtor could pay, yet both were forgiven. When Jeff read the parable in his class, a man of influence and authority expressed deep discomfort. He'd considered himself a righteous person—a church-attending, good-doing saint. How could a wanton sinner end up loving the Lord more? He found the notion offensive. It seemed unfair. Yet Christ confirmed Simon's interpretation, saying, "Thou has rightly judged."

Jeff turned his palms up and shrugged his shoulders, reenacting his response to the agitated class member, as if to say, "Hey, I didn't write it. I'm just reading it." We both smiled.

Christ told Simon, "Her sins, which are many, are forgiven; for she loved much: but to whom little is forgiven, the same loveth little." Then he turned back to the woman and said, "Thy sins are forgiven . . . Thy faith hath saved thee; go in peace"

(Luke 7:47-50, KJV).

Christ's forgiveness was immediate and unconditional, like the feelings of sanctification Jeff had experienced in the presence of Divinity. Christ didn't say to the woman, "Thy repentance hath saved thee." He said, "Thy faith hath saved thee." Who can say what this generous, unexpected, undeserved gift of forgiveness wrought in the life of that woman and those around her? What great things might she have gone on to do because of that ennobling act? Perhaps she went on to forgive others, enabling them to do the same. Some might argue that if we all had the faith to forgive one another, God would likewise forgive us, as described in the Lord's Prayer. Then there'd be no need to repent because there'd be no unforgiven offenses.

Jeff and I had a lively discussion that day. Lunch went long into the afternoon. One of the things I loved about our discussions was that we both came with an open schedule and we let things flow where they would, and for as long as it took. We'd often go for three or four hours. I don't recall with certainty our discussion, but I suspect it was then that I shared two of my contrasting near-life experiences: one agonizing, one exalting.

In one of my darkest hours, in mid-April, just two weeks after meeting Jeff—in a deeper, more wrenching horror than I'd ever experienced—a voice I knew came into my soul and whispered, "this is what it feels like to groan in the spirit and be troubled."

The words were familiar, but I had to look them up. They described the feelings of Christ when Mary and Martha lamented the death of their brother Lazerus and failed to comprehend the power of God to raise him from death. They failed to believe or understand. "Jesus groaned in the spirit, and was troubled" (John 11:33, KJV). Then he wept. Then he raised Lazerus.

I had a taste of those feelings. It was a horrible, soul-rending sadness. It was a sadness for others more than for myself, a deep sorrow for reasons I can't explain here or attempt to describe in print. I concluded it was part of the vicarious learning I'd long ago prayed for. I was still being led through others' experiences and the accompanying feelings—feelings so deep and visceral they return whenever I think of that night.

In brilliant contrast, I also enjoyed the opposite extreme. On a separate night, in preparation for evening prayer, I felt a light embrace me, starting in the center of my being and spreading to the tip of each extremity. It consumed every fragment of my body and spirit and wrapped me in unbounded love. I felt at one with all of creation and free from every hint of resentment toward another soul. This time the voice said, "Thy sins are forgiven thee."

There was no apparent reason or timing for the gift. That's why it was so powerful. I wasn't expecting it. I could not have expected it because I hadn't earned it. I couldn't earn it. I didn't deserve it. I had no reason to think that night would be different from any other.

One reason I felt so deeply grateful for the gift I'd received was that it reset my world. My memory is both a gift and a curse. The same memory that once held onto 350 pages of scripture now holds onto too many missteps and regrets and replays them too often—the worse the memory, the more frequently it rolls into the queue. I see the wrongs I've done over and over again, relentlessly, mercilessly. Even when I repent and find forgiveness, the memory doesn't evaporate. God promised ancient Israel *he* would remember their sins no more. That godly gift of forgetting has not been granted to me. But, now, with the comprehensive gift of forgiveness, the memories are no longer drenched in guilt. I felt profoundly grateful for the ineffable love and sanctification that night. I wept.

Because of how it felt to be unconditionally forgiven, I wanted to unconditionally forgive others. In my little way, to the extent possible, I wanted to give that gift. It's hard for me at times, and some days I'm more forgiving than others. It depends on the traffic, the weather, and the disposition of others around me, but it shouldn't. If I could forgive one other person and make them feel a glint of what I'd felt, they would forgive someone else for the same reason. We would all move a little closer to being one. Jeff and I have talked about these things many times. He's better at it than I.

Messages of forgiveness don't come when we expect them.

Take the palsied man who was lowered through the roof into the presence of Christ in hopes of being physically healed. "And when [Christ] saw their faith, he said unto him, Man, thy sins are forgiven thee" (Luke 5:18-20, KJV).

Discerning the thoughts of his offended observers, Christ asked:

> What reason ye in your hearts? Whether is easier, to say, Thy sins be forgiven thee; or to say, Rise up and walk? But that ye may know that the Son of man hath power upon earth to forgive sins, (he said unto the sick of the palsy,) I say unto thee, Arise, and take up thy couch, and go into thine house. And immediately he rose up before them, and took up that whereon he lay, and departed to his own house, glorifying God. (Luke 5:21-26, KJV)

That's what happened to Jeff Olsen. The things he experienced while his body slumped in a hospital bed sanctified him. Then he rose up and walked. And he's been glorifying God ever since. He wouldn't like me saying that, but this is my book, so I can say it.

I believe Christ demonstrated to the man with palsy that forgiveness and physical healing are two sides of the same coin— not that illness is a consequence of sin, but that healing the soul includes healing both spirit and body. James suggested the same connection when he wrote, "the prayer of faith shall save the sick, and the Lord shall raise him up; and if he have committed sins, they shall be forgiven" (James 5:14-15, KJV).

Victor Hugo offered much to ponder in *Les Misérables*. Clearly, Jean Valjean had not repented of stealing the silverware, but Monsieur Bienvenu gave him the candlesticks also and whispered, "Jean Valjean, my brother: you belong no longer to evil, but to good. It is your soul that I am buying for you. I withdraw it from dark thoughts and from the spirit of perdition, and I give it to God!" Bienvenu's forgiveness in advance of repentance saved a soul. It changed Jean Valjean and allowed him to go out and do likewise.

There was a time when I rarely read fiction. I thought I had better things to do in the real world. Then I realized some souls are so sensitive they can come to their defining moments through fiction. Their circumstances can be fictional and still get them to the feelings they need to empathize. I felt it reading *Les Miserables*. Art can do the same thing. My love of good literature was boosted when I realized that Christ taught almost exclusively by asking the right questions and telling stories (parables).

I think Monsieur Bienvenu's message to Jean Valjean is the same message I was taught when I received the impression to speak to those souls in prison about forgiveness rather than repentance. A preoccupation with repentance risks developing an expectation of being forgiven, as though I'd earned it. It also risks developing an expectation that others repent to my standard. I believe that's one reason the man in Jeff's Sunday school class was offended. It's easy for us to think the sinner who washed her Lord's feet just hadn't repented enough. But Christ's parable made it explicitly clear that forgiveness may come in advance of repentance.

People who embrace the idea of Christ's Atonement (and I realize that many do not) sometimes talk of it as eternity's most unselfish act. Ironically, they also often talk about it in the most selfish way. They speak of "*my* personal Savior" and say, "*my* Savior died for *my* sins." As true as those statements may be, they only describe a fragment of the Atonement. Wouldn't it be much better if those who believed in the Atonement—and I am one who does believe—said, "*our* Savior died for *our* sins"? If I more fully embraced that view of Christ's Atonement—that it has been accomplished, and that my neighbor's sins have been forgiven—I can more easily set aside the inclination to judge the repentance of those around me. I can just let it all go.

And what if Christ's Atonement was about something much larger than repentance and forgiveness and paying the price for others' sins? What if it was also about taking on the burdens of his people in the perfect act of empathy, enabling him to understand them perfectly and help them in their trials? And, what if the Atonement of Christ, like every other act in his mortal ministry, was an example for me to follow? I once thought that last question sounded blasphemous. I no longer feel that way. That Christ did it perfectly and comprehensively does not preclude me from picking up a tiny fragment and muddling along doing my best, learning as I go.

Thinking less selfishly about repentance might be equally liberating. Some say we have no need to repent. I can't go that far, not even after the unconditional forgiveness I've received on more than one occasion. I make mistakes and I need to do my part to rectify them. Repentance is a good thing.

I would also say, however, my larger and nobler obligation is to forgive. It can be hard to forgive, but failing to forgive impedes my progress. Conversely, it's harder for others to forgive me if I wrong them and make no effort to repent. I don't prevent them from forgiving, but I make it harder. What if I thought of repentance as a gift I offer to one I love to assist him or her in their forgiveness of me? To be sure, repentance helps me, but what if I stopped thinking so selfishly? Repentance is a gift I give to help others progress. I know that's a radical notion, but stew on it for a while.

I think of repentance as arithmetic and forgiveness as calculus. If I ruminate on my times tables until I get them perfect, I'll never do algebra, geometry, trigonometry, or calculus. Math is essential, but regardless of how much I practice basic math, I'll occasionally make a mistake. That shouldn't stop me, however, from moving on to more advanced concepts. I should not obsess over perfect math to the exclusion of everything it opens to my view.

The same is true for repentance and forgiveness. When I obsess on repentance—on me—I focus inwardly at the expense of the much more ennobling and unselfish practice of forgiving. I'll make mistakes—that's why I'm here—but focusing on forgiveness will elevate my sights and my service.

The master of a vineyard hired laborers early in the morning and throughout the day. When it came time to pay them, he compensated them equally regardless of the hours they'd worked (Matthew 20:1-16, KJV). While many have offered various interpretations, I like an idea suggested to me by a friend. Perhaps they were all compensated equally because they were being rewarded for what they *became* rather than for what they *did*. Perhaps I'll receive my ultimate reward, not for what I've done, but for what I've become. That feels right to me. We all become at different rates and according to individualized plans. It is not about what we do; it's about who we are.

Apocalypse is the Greek word for revelation. Literally, it means to unveil. From my perspective, one of the greatest truths unveiled in the book of Revelation tells us something about our true status with Heaven. It's found in chapter three. I shared this with a Catholic friend as we debated which religious tradition infuses its adherents with the largest supply of guilt. She insisted it was Catholicism. Growing up Mormon, I think they're in the race. I had her read verse five. She promptly launched into a discussion about how we must labor to get our names recorded in the Lamb's Book of Life. I could hear all of her childhood indoctrination resurfacing. I asked her to read the verse again: "He that overcometh, the same shall be clothed in white raiment; and I will not blot out his name out of the book of life" (Revelation 3:5, KJV).

The light went on, and she smiled widely. "My name is already there," she said.

"All of our names," I added. "They can't be blotted out unless they are already there in the first place. We're not laboring to earn our salvation. It's already been given to us. What we should be laboring toward is helping others come to the same realization. Then people can stop worrying about themselves and start helping others."

The next day my friend told me of a conversation she'd had with her sister that night. Her sister wasn't surprised by the verse from Revelation. She'd known about it. In fact, she'd known a person who'd shared his NDE with her and told her he'd seen his own name recorded in the book of life.

I was thrilled when I received my message of forgiveness, but it was not a one-time event. I've received that joy more than once. I need it, and often. When I've felt forgiven, I want to forgive others. I don't want them to repent; I just want to forgive. I know intellectually there's something perfect and divine deep inside me, but I struggle to comport my mortal counterpart with my inner soul. I make mistakes and I feel unworthy. Increasingly, I realize those judgments are coming from me, not from above. Perhaps I need to learn to forgive myself.

17

BUSINESS

Jeff was always willing: willing to go, to learn, to live, to forgive. He was always a good example for me. As we moved into the thick of the holiday season, we continued our conversations. We talked about the importance of pondering and learning through meditation. Some of our best conversations followed our most instructive moments of solitude. Meditative practices are widely discussed in the context of Hindu, Buddhist, Taoist, Jewish, Christian, Islamic, and Native American traditions. Unfortunately, they're discussed more than they're practiced. Learning to listen is learning to live, but it's hard to listen when someone is talking to you. It's even harder when you're the one talking. Jeff and I have both quoted the psalmist, "Be still, and know that I am God" (Psalms 46:10, KJV).

I had one of those still moments while sitting in the lobby of a downtown hotel, one of my favorite spots to ponder. Even though people passed through the space, it was quiet and peaceful. I watched small children play around an enormous Christmas tree that extended well beyond the first floor ceiling and through the opening that led to the mezzanine.

I wondered how these souls had possessed such vast knowledge before their birth and now knew so little. Then I realized another purpose for the veil in which I am wrapped. It's a protection for me; it protects me from my own knowledge. It allows me to recover my pre-earth knowledge, a tiny fragment at a time, as I learn and grow and become accountable for it. I couldn't be accountable for all that knowledge as an immature and errant mortal; it would destroy me. I remember it bit by bit as I grow and learn. When I'm ready, it comes, as Isaiah said, "precept upon precept; line upon line . . . here a little, and there a little" (Isaiah 28:10, KJV).

As I pondered what I'd come to understand, a friend approached and asked how I had time to just sit and do nothing. The heavens had just opened to me and taught me something profound, and he thought I was doing nothing. We were good friends, so I knew he'd understand when I said, "I'm not doing nothing; I'm learning." We both smiled.

Jeff and I talked about what we had once known and what we now know, or, more particularly, what we remember. Jeff's NDE had commenced before his severely injured body had even been extricated from the mangled wreckage. He went to a place of joy and soon realized his excruciating pain had gone. "It was familiar," he'd later write. "It was home. My natural senses were magnified to a greater degree. There were a million questions racing through my head, but as soon as I thought of a question, the answer was immediately there. There was an ancient awareness, as if I had always been in this place" (*I Knew Their Hearts*, 31).

That was his published account, refined by ten years of contemplation and an editor. I got the raw version in 1997. We simply talked about how he could possibly know so much. How could he have his own answers to a million questions? His experience was not unique. I've heard Dannion Brinkley and

Eben Alexander both talk about how liberating death was to their spirits and how their mortal bodies functioned as filters. I heard one person familiar with NDEs say, "All of your answers are within you." Without the filters, our knowledge is vast and our recall immediate. I've had my own experiences. I know it's true.

Jeff and I discussed the scope of our spiritual knowledge in the New Testament context we'd relied on as young missionaries. In his first epistle, John told his followers, "ye have an unction from the Holy One, and ye know all things" (1 John 2:20, KJV). That's heady stuff. It sounds almost blasphemous to tell someone "ye know all things," but that's what John wrote. It sounds less blasphemous if one believes Christ's declaration: "Ye are gods" (John 10:34, KJV).

An unction is another way of saying an anointing. As mentioned in a previous chapter, every soul on earth has had an anointing. When he was baptized, Christ was further "anointed . . . with the Holy Ghost" (Acts 10:38, KJV). John went on to write, "the anointing which ye have received of him abideth in you, and ye need not that any man teach you: but as the same anointing teacheth you of all things, and is truth, and is no lie" (1 John 2:27, KJV).

When spirits leave their bodies or otherwise pierce the veil, they find instantaneous answers to questions because they already possess the knowledge and no longer have a veil to prevent them from remembering. Jeff was told things he didn't have the words to describe, yet it didn't feel to him like learning; it was more like remembering. It flowed through him. It was the same experience I'd had with Tamara, when knowledge just rested easily in our common spiritual space and invited me to partake. It was common knowledge, not something I had to struggle to learn.

Spirit guides, guardian angels, and other messengers may draw back the veil and help us remember. In fact, in Christianity, the process is so important, a member of the godhead is expressly tasked to do just that. The Holy Ghost will "teach you all things, and bring all things to your remembrance" (John 14:26, KJV). One way to find knowledge, then, is to look beyond the veil— deep inside yourself, with or without dying—and remember.

The truths I'm describing transcend religion. Jeff and I conversed in our shared vocabulary, but we could have had the same conversation in almost any religious or cultural construct if we'd simply used different words. Our experiences were not religious; they were spiritual.

Sometimes the direction of our spiritual journey is counterintuitive. It's not an outward trek across oceans and continents. It's an inward journey to find one's self. When mortals enter man-made temples, they move to the center—sometimes circumambulating and ascending—to the symbolic seat of all truth and glory. In Israel, the mercy seat was located in the center of the tabernacle behind the veil—not at the periphery, not in the courtyard. People do not enter a temple and then go to the window, draw the drape, and look outward for answers. They move to the center.

The same is true within my divine temple—this body that is the tabernacle of my eternal spirit. The seat of my knowledge is within me, deep in the center, behind the veil. Before I look outward for answers, I should look within. I should find a way to part the veil and remember what I've previously known and now forgotten.

Prayer, meditation, and other practices that assist us in communing with Heaven are paths to greater light. Notwithstanding the eternal, expansive, and nigh on infinite knowledge of human souls, I am here to learn yet more and to gain experience and help others to do the same.

Scott called me not long before Christmas. His baptism was rapidly approaching. He asked if I'd attend and speak. The season must have influenced my topic. When I spoke, I drew upon Dickens to reflect what I'd learned in recent years and to convey what I thought would help us all do better.

As the ghost of Marley lamented the selfishness of his mortal follies, Scrooge countered, "But you were always a good man of business, Jacob." Marley took no comfort. He wrung his hands and cried out, "Mankind was my business. The common welfare was my business; charity, mercy, forbearance, and benevolence, were, all, my business. The dealings of my trade were but a drop of water in the comprehensive ocean of my business!"[4]

I concluded my remarks and I sat down. A kind voice whispered, "Thou hast saved a soul." I looked around. No one was speaking. I began to squirm and contemplate what seemed like yet another blasphemous thought. Who was speaking to me? Why? How? All I did was offer a few remarks at a friend's baptism. I hadn't saved anybody. Humans don't save souls. God does that.

As my mind raced, Scott took the pulpit. With a crack in his voice, he said, "Jeff, you saved my life." He turned from the congregation and looked at me for an eternity of seconds. I sat there dumbfounded. I couldn't look away; I couldn't say anything. Perhaps we all do more than we realize.

---

[4] *A Christmas Carol*, Charles Dickens, 1812-1870.

18

EMPATHY

December 30, 1997, was approaching—Stan's fortieth birthday. He'd been dead for twenty-five years, but I'd become increasingly aware that he was not gone. Sometimes it felt like he'd stand near the veil and introduce people, as if he knew what I needed to learn and who could teach it to me. In retrospect, I think I missed his presence for a while. As I grew into what I was experiencing and learned to ask the right questions, his involvement became more obvious. He once apologized for something he'd done in our childhood. I couldn't resist forgiving him. The offense had been so small. I felt bad for the burden he'd carried.

I'd felt the same burden for years. A few weeks later, I approached my younger sister and similarly asked her forgiveness for what I thought was a terrible childhood misadventure. She said, "I forgive you; don't ever think about it again." We can ease one another's burdens simply by forgiving one another. I can give that gift freely and earnestly, and I should give it more often.

Early in December, I'd engaged a police sketch artist I knew. I provided pictures, and he produced an age-progressed image of Stan. I gave 40-year-old Stan to my parents for Christmas. The image still hangs on their wall. When I see it, I'm grateful for his ongoing help and encouragement. Sometimes I wonder if Tamara played a role in reconnecting us.

My experiences in the ER were frequent that winter, like a spiritual crescendo. In early December, I encountered a woman who was just becoming aware of her existence outside of her body, but soon her presence began to fade. Then she was gone. I looked over to see the resuscitation team had restored her heartbeat. She wasn't gone at all. She had simply returned to her body and was again behind her veil.

Late in the month, a couple came into the department from a serious car crash. Their daughter, who'd died at the scene, accompanied them, just like Tamara had accompanied Jeff. For some reason, it didn't feel right for me to say anything, so I left it alone.

In January, I assisted another physician in the care of a young boy, struggling for an hour to stabilize him. I felt his presence throughout the ordeal and pled with Heaven for direction. None came. When he died, I wondered if I had somehow failed.

Spiritual experiences continued outside the ER as well. I met regularly with Rachel, who was emerging from her struggles. She shared visions from her childhood that stunned me. I wondered how someone could experience such things and still struggle. Then I looked at myself. It's strange—isn't it?—how we can see things clearly in others while missing them in ourselves. I was glad to see her countenance brightening. One of our visits came after a funeral for a flight nurse who'd died in a helicopter crash. Rachel told me how much the nurse's widow had appreciated a letter I'd written. I'd offered what encouragement I could and cautioned her about asking, *Why?* In my experience, when someone dies, asking why rarely provides answers or comfort; it only spirals us into the abyss. The answer is always the same:

Because.

It was about that time that I apparently needed another reminder of the importance of not judging. I'd learned it on many occasions, such as when I'd spoken at the prison, but I needed reminding. Janet would teach me. She was a vivacious nurse that had encouraged and taught me as a young physician.

Janet was one of the most beautiful women I'd ever known. She taught me something wonderful without even knowing. Her spiritual appearance was every bit as beautiful as her physical. She had a brilliant, gleaming countenance. If I struggled to see god in others, I never failed to see it in her. The only thing that exceeded her beauty was her compassionate personality. I wasn't the only person who felt that way; I've heard many people say similar things.

One seeming contradiction I couldn't understand about Janet was how she could preserve such a stunning spiritual presence while choosing to live outside the moral boundaries she'd once embraced. I knew what those boundaries were because she'd told me. I later learned she'd made some of her decisions because of the way her father had treated her. She was doing things she'd been taught were wrong, and that *she* believed were wrong, but somehow maintained her spiritual countenance. How was that possible?

Her life was none of my business. She could live how she wished. I didn't begrudge her choices, but I still had the question. I prayed about it. The answer contradicted every prejudice I'd clung to. Perhaps I was a little too much like the man in Jeff's Sunday school class.

"Because of who she is," I was told. "And because I love her so much."

Whatever choices Janet was making that may have seemed wrong to me, or to her father or to her, they were her choices, and she was on her own journey. I didn't know who she was spiritually except that I knew she had a divine nature and heritage. Now I'd learned something that should have been obvious to me, something of how much God loved her. That jolted me back to reality.

The experience reminded me that judging others impedes every good thing I might try to accomplish. When I judge another's path, I demonstrate a selfish lack of trust in God. I climb up on my soapbox of arrogance and proclaim that God loves me so much he custom designed a path for my greatest good, but he hasn't done the same for others. When I judge others, I judge God.

Janet and I were such good friends, and she was so open with her life decisions, I felt I could share what I'd learned. She received it gratefully. Tears streamed down her face as if she already knew but just needed to hear it again—as if I was telling her something she'd already received directly from the Source. Her response was authentic and deeply moving, but not something I feel comfortable including here. When our conversation touched on prayer, she told me she hadn't prayed in years. Four days later, she came back to me, hugged me, and told me she was praying again.

I still fall into the trap of judging, but Janet reminded me why I shouldn't.

Later the same day, I found myself in the hospital cafeteria. I walked toward the cashier with a tray full of food and glanced down to see a boy who seemed about five or six years old. I looked just in time to see his hot dog slide out of the bun, off the plate, over the edge of the tray, and onto the floor, leaving two streaks along the path: one yellow, one red. His eyes inched up to an angry and disappointed look from the man I assumed was his father. The man didn't say anything. He just glared and walked away, back toward the grill.

I could almost see the tears forming in the boy's eyes. I could feel them in mine. I felt his devastation. I wanted to pick him up and hug him and tell him everything was fine. *It's just a hot dog.* That's what I wanted to say, but I couldn't. I felt like any attempt to show compassion would only inflame the situation further. I could feel the anger he'd endured in past encounters in less public places. I pulled some napkins from my tray and handed them to the boy while offering the kindest look I could muster. I didn't feel like I could say it out loud, but I wanted him to know I loved him. I wanted him to know that someone loved him, that he was loved. He looked at me as if he understood. Then he leaned down and began to wipe the catsup and mustard from the floor. I still wonder if I should have done more.

There was always more I could do. One of my challenges was finding the balance between what I *could* do and what I *should* do. Heather was a nurse I'd known since I was an intern. We'd talked about many things over the years, both spiritual and medical. Nurses teach naïve interns a lot. Like Janet, Heather continued to teach me life lessons even after I was an attending physician.

Heather was kind and soft-spoken for the most part, a single mother struggling to provide for her family. I recall one night, however, when I heard an interaction behind a curtain that showcased another facet of her personality, one that I came to love. Her patient had slept for hours, metabolizing the alcohol that had led to his visit. Then he awoke and began to relieve himself. He simply rolled on his side and let loose through the side-rail of his gurney. The splashing sounds had drawn Heather to the room.

"What the hell are you doing?" she exclaimed, her voice louder and in a distinctly different tone than I'd previously heard. "I don't come into your house and pee on your floor!" She continued her rant as I started to laugh. She and the patient were the only two people in the area, except for me on the other side of the curtain. She concluded by threatening to cut off a certain body part if he repeated his offense. By the time she emerged from the other side of the curtain, I was about to fall of my chair. We still laugh about it.

I'd extended financial assistance to Heather's family in a time of need. I thought she was the only one who knew. On the same day Janet told me she'd resumed her prayers, I got a note from Heather's teenage son, thanking me for the help. Sometimes we get little reminders to encourage us through difficult times. Janet and Heather's son brightened that day for me.

In 1995, less than a week after experiencing a taste of the horror Rebekah had felt when Don died, I'd had a two-hour visit with Heather. Like Susan, Heather's husband had died of cancer and left her with young children to care for. Unlike Susan, Heather's husband had died slowly through years of chemo and unnumbered prayers. I'd wondered many times whether it was harder for Rebekah to lose her companion without the opportunity to say goodbye or for Heather to lose her sweetheart slowly, all the while feeling her petitions for his recovery would be granted. Both felt betrayed by their God. Both thought the other's situation would have been better.

Heather and I talked a lot about how to begin to feel again after immeasurable pain. At that time, I hadn't yet experienced my epiphany about attachment disorder. I didn't think I had a problem with feelings or the lack thereof. Over the years, Heather taught me otherwise. I came to understand that the good comes with the bad. Opening myself to Rebekah's pain would eventually open me to greater joy as well. Heather gradually helped me feel the smaller things more deeply, like a hot dog on the floor of a hospital cafeteria and a young boy's self-worth smeared across the tiles in red and yellow. It doesn't sound so small when it's described like that, does it? Empathy is a painful thing at times. It breaks your heart when you least expect it.

19

PAIN

By early March of 1998, Rachel was back in sync with her spiritual self. It was good to see her out of the darkness. Julian and I hadn't been in any fast cars for a while, but he was also doing well, as was Rebekah. They each sent letters when I needed them most. "Perhaps I needed some reassurance that my life makes a difference to someone," I wrote that evening. The rest of the journal entry was morose. It must have been a bad day. Sometimes I'm better at helping others feel their self-worth and their relationship with Heaven than feeling it myself.

March 31 was looming close. Anniversaries are tough, especially the first one, and I knew Jeff's one-year mark was approaching. I called to see how he was doing. I didn't know then that he'd met Tonya that day, or what would become of their relationship. Perhaps Jeff knew she would help him heal. I heard something buoyant in his voice. I summarized our call: "He is doing remarkably well. He is very in-tune with the Spirit and constantly being tutored." Jeff and Tonya would soon marry. They're still together.

Throughout our first year of friendship, Jeff was more attuned to spiritual matters than most people. That comes as no surprise to those who have been close to NDEs. Walking with angels changes people, sometimes heightening their latent spiritual gifts. It puts them in closer proximity to the veil and makes them more inclined to recognize those moments when eternity peeks through. Jeff had more revelatory dreams after his NDE. I didn't know him before the accident, but I was impressed with the peacefulness that settled upon him in the last half of 1997. He'd plowed through the physical hardships: getting a new leg, learning to walk again, healing his abdominal injuries, and regaining his independence. He still had a limp and more healing to come, but he was moving forward. His spirit had healed too, but that also was unfinished. What he'd experienced while out of his body gave him a framework—a path and a destination—but he still had to make the journey. Journeys are often fraught with pain.

People encounter pain in different ways and in different places. I was still an intern when my attending physician said, "Go see that patient in room seven." I dutifully marched off to the other end of the department.

The patient in room seven had arrived by ambulance, in a cervical collar and strapped to a backboard, after falling from a moving vehicle. I saw a beautiful young woman in a purple suede mini skirt and matching vest. The stiletto heel of one shoe was broken off. Her other shoe remained on the road somewhere near her missing oversized earring. The color of her outfit trailed off in various directions, down her arms and legs. Rainwater had leached inexpensive dye from the leather and followed gravity. The purple streamers went in several directions because her body had assumed numerous positions between the time she'd hit the wet pavement and when she'd arrived in the ER. All the lines were the same color except those extending from her eyes. Those were black from the mascara that stained her tears.

Her knees and elbows had superficial abrasions but her x-rays were negative. Fortunately, the truck was moving slowly when she'd bailed out. Her tears were not from physical pain. They originated from deeper injuries. Her story was haunting.

Some "John" had picked her up downtown. He spewed out increasingly disturbing comments until he slowed to make a left-hand turn, at the same time asking her to call him "Daddy." She opened the door at the point of maximal centrifugal force and flew from the vehicle. As far as she was concerned, anything would be better than what he had in mind.

She no longer went by the name of Mindy. That's what her father had called her as he sexually abused her for five of her teenage years. His abuse only stopped because she left home. Still a teenager, the thought of calling her latest abuser "Daddy" caused something deep inside to snap.

Sadly, her history came as no surprise. I've never taken care of a prostitute, an exotic dancer, or anyone else in the sex-trade that was not abused as a child. They may exist, but I haven't met one. The depth of injury and the consequences of abuse are inestimable. Generations suffer. Society stands aghast and seems almost impotent. The scope of the problem is terrifying.

One reason abuse—physical, sexual, emotional, whatever—is so difficult to combat or prevent is because the seeds are planted so early. While abuse crosses all religious, socioeconomic and cultural boundaries, studies have identified two risk factors: abused boys are more likely to abuse their wives and children; and abused girls are much more likely to choose men who will abuse them. Abuse, though painful, is linked in some distorted way to the love a child should have received and the love they later try to embrace. Unchecked, the fruit of abuse is another generation of torture.

Hurting others is just one consequence of being abused. Hurting one's self is even more prevalent. Misplaced blame, shame, and anger find vent in self-harm. For many, the outlet is addiction. For some, it's death. For all, it's a desire to end the pain.

Most souls are searching for peace. Relatively few find it. To suggest a solution in brief anecdotes could only trivialize the problem and sound cliché. What impresses me—what changes me—is the realization that so many people are in so much pain. Pain, it seems, is the lowest common denominator in humanity. Pain, more than anything else, makes us all alike. What tears us apart is the naïve arrogance of thinking our own situation—our own brand of pain—is somehow different, somehow more important than someone else's.

Pain is what I see so often in ER patients. I've cared for alcoholics, workaholics, drug addicts, compulsive gamblers and sex addicts. I've taken care of abusers and the victims of abuse, and the parents, children, and siblings of each.

One humble gentleman told me of the pain he'd silently carried for decades. He'd never spoken of it since the day it happened. His pain grew from an entirely different form of violence. He'd landed on Iwo Jima. As a medic, he stood in ankle-deep blood and looked about in utter helplessness. He wept as he unburdened his soul for the first time in half a century. I was the first person he'd spoken to about it.

I often wonder about the pain that afflicts us all, that makes us one. Sometimes it's nothing more or less than a spiritual homesickness—a gnawing spiritual hunger for the divine glory we once enjoyed. Sometimes, of course, it is much more. Sometimes it's a frank and deep-seated depression requiring expert medical intervention. But when it is that spiritual loneliness, and when we come to see that longing in one another, the cure becomes obvious.

After twenty years in the ER, I sat with a tearful young man who admitted he just didn't know how to deal with the pain any longer. The first anniversary of his brother's untimely death had just passed. The grief interfered with his work, his relationships, and his ability to function in life. He had nowhere to go and no one to help him. He felt as though no one could understand. He felt absolutely alone.

I knew little of the young man's life and nothing of his religious background. I knew, however, that he was in pain. I had an inkling of what he needed. His whole countenance changed when he heard me say, "I remember how I felt when my brother died."

As I shared a few simple thoughts and feelings, his tears stopped, his back straightened, and his shoulders squared as though an unseen physical burden was being lifted from his being. I hadn't taken his problem away. I couldn't do that. All I did was offer a little perspective and the realization that he was not as alone as he had felt. As I spoke, hope returned to his face and confidence to his eyes.

I hadn't learned such treatment in medical school. I learned it from the souls who wandered in and out of my life. I ordered no labs or x-rays. He needed no medication. All he needed was someone who cared. The fact that I could speak from experience helped, but the common thread was pain, and the common cure, compassion. In that way, to the extent we are willing, we can all heal one another.

The mists of darkness and the pains of life are inevitable. They're on the path we all must tread. Trying to avoid them through drugs, alcohol, sexual exploitation, or any number of other destructive behaviors only takes us away from the ultimate happiness we truly desire and the rewards that await an authentic life. All the distractions and substitutes are temporary. Love and empathy are real and eternal.

Jeff suffered incomprehensible pain: physical, emotional, and spiritual. Fifteen years after his adventure beyond the veil, with a new wife and two more sons, he wrote, "I expected my new wife to fill me up and make me whole. I expected my children to heal me, and in many ways they all have, but looking outward for wholeness was a losing and painful battle . . . Not until I remembered the divinity within myself did I become whole."[5] I saw that transition. I saw Jeff Olsen process his pain and realize his divine nature.

---

[5] *Beyond Mile Marker 80* (Plain Sight Publishing, Springville, Utah, 2014), 101.

20

REMEMBER

On a beautiful summer day on the island of Corregidor I walked the understated promenade from a small tourist road to the rotunda of the Pacific War Memorial. The view was expansive, and a gentle breeze carried the scent of the sea over the summit. The place offered a solemn feeling.

Suddenly I became aware of the presence of tens of thousands of souls. Barriers of time and distance disappeared. I could feel their presence as much as see them. The vastness of the gathering was overwhelming.

I'd visited the Manila American Cemetery and Memorial the previous day. I'd walked amid the 17,000 headstones and studied the mosaics on the walls of the memorial where 36,000 names honored those whose remains were never recovered. I knew the Battle of Leyte Gulf was the largest naval engagement in the history of the world and that Corregidor sat in the mouth of

Manila Bay adjacent to the Bataan Peninsula, where the horrors of the infamous Death March had unfolded. In a moment, I comprehended the presence of them all, and more. In the enormity of the experience, I wept.

A few people passed without slowing. From all I could tell, the vision was mine alone. I called upon wisdom I'd learned from the Apostle Paul. When a resurrected Christ visited him, Paul asked two questions: Who are you? and What would you have me do? I've found those questions useful when I've encountered spiritual feelings.

I silently asked my legion of visitors, though I felt I already knew, "Who are you?" Their response, silent to all but me: "We are many."

The concourses of souls seemed endless, all against the backdrop of sea and sky. Despite their violent deaths, they enveloped me in their sense of peace and in the full measure of their contentment. They were there for me. How could that be? How could they all care about me? Why would they gather in such a way?

Moved by the feeling that there was purpose in this miracle, I asked, "What would you have me do?"

They answered my second question as quickly as the first: "Remember."

That's all they said. That was the only thing they asked me to do. Because the communication was pure and complete, I knew their thoughts and feelings. I knew that all they wanted me to do was remember their sacrifice and the marvelous gift they had given the world.

I'd known Jeff for about seven years by then. We met less frequently, but I often thought of him when the heavens opened because we'd shared so much. Six months after my trip to the Philippines, we shared lunch and a long conversation. We talked about Corregidor and the two questions I'd asked. I know he has since asked the same two questions during some of his spiritual experiences. Asking is so crucial to learning.

We can forget our spiritual experiences if we bury them and walk away. Tens of thousands of soldiers from WWII reminded me how important it is to remember. Spiritual experiences, as marvelous as they may be, are usually scattered over time, sometimes years apart. It's easy to get discouraged or forget. Writing this book, I was grateful for my journal. It seems I remember the bad better than the good. Some entries were brief or cryptic but buoyed my spirit. I wish I'd written more.

The day after I returned from the Philippines was Friday the thirteenth of June, my seventeenth wedding anniversary, and a special one. Sheila and I were married on Friday the thirteenth. This was the first time our anniversary had fallen on a Friday since our wedding in 1986. We celebrated in a strange way.

On an early news program, I noted that Salt Lake City was hosting a reunion of the survivors of Bataan and Corregidor. Sheila and I promptly headed to the event. We entered cautiously, not sure how we'd be received. When I told these aging veterans where I'd been and how much I appreciated their service, they welcomed me like an old friend. They were warm and gracious and proceeded to share their stories. Sheila and I listened for hours. These living veterans confirmed the message of their dead comrades; they simply wanted us to remember.

Every time I think about those experiences, I feel the veil thin and separate, and I enjoy a hint of the vision I had on Corregidor. When I remember, it opens the door to near-life experiences.

21

FEELINGS

My patient was barely more than a teenager. He squirmed impatiently as he tried to persuade me to let him get up and go home. His story sounded innocent enough, and he seemed quite well. He told me how he'd slowed his motorcycle and swerved to avoid the car that had stopped abruptly in front of him. He'd laid his bike on its side, slid it across the road and bumped into the curb at low speed. Wearing full leathers and a helmet, he seemed to have escaped serious injury.

Following protocol, paramedics had placed him in a cervical collar and strapped him to a backboard. By the time he arrived in the emergency department, he was uncomfortable and wanted to get up. I looked at his helmet. There was hardly a scratch. He'd not lost consciousness. He had no evidence of injury, not even a headache. I was about to accommodate his request and let him leave when I had one of those feelings—one of those sudden sickening feelings, when your heart and stomach exchange places and dance out an unsettling warning that you're on the verge of a serious mistake. I couldn't justify my decision by any published medical criteria, but I decided to scan his head. He was well enough to joke with me about the x-rays we both thought were unnecessary.

Fifteen minutes later, as I looked at his scan, I had that same sickening feeling in reverse—you know, that brief glimpse of the sinking blackness that might have been, and a sense of relief that some ineffable influence had changed your course before it was too late. His brain was displaced under the pressure of accumulating arterial blood inside his skull. His scan had the classic appearance of an epidural hematoma, with one added twist: he was bleeding so briskly you could actually see swirls of blood on the scan.

I went back to talk with him. He was still conversant, but drowsy. Twenty minutes later, a neurosurgeon drained the hematoma. As dramatic as that sounds, it was a relatively benign procedure and my patient would be back on his motorcycle soon. Had I sent him home, he would almost certainly have died before midnight.

I seldom feel I've saved a life in the ER. Things are rarely so dramatic. When I think of that young man, any inclination to celebrate my success is tempered by two things: a sobering realization of how close I came to doing the wrong thing, and a deep humbling gratitude for an unseen intervention.

I wonder if some part of my patient—some part more than mortal—knew what was happening and communicated it to me in a way that words fail to describe. I'm inclined to believe there was something more than science at work that night. Had I strictly followed medical protocols, I would have sent him home without the scan. It's happened to me too many times to count. Sometimes, if I can just quiet all the distractions, some influence helps me do the right thing.

22

HUMILITY

Sheila and I celebrated our twenty-fifth wedding anniversary in Jackson Hole, Wyoming. My friend, who was also a physician, called to tell me his wife had been in a horrible accident in Hawaii. Shelli was unconscious in a hospital 3,000 miles away. A pit opened in my stomach and swallowed every happy thought. He described her brain injury and the rest of her medical condition in great detail. Every bit of medical information enlarged the hole in my belly. The best possible outcome seemed to be that she would die quickly without further suffering and before her cardiopulmonary condition stabilized to leave her in a permanent vegetative state. Before Shelli's husband disconnected, he asked me to pray for her.

From all my medical training, and more than twenty years of experience, I knew the prognosis was dismal. Shelli's husband was being pressured to discontinue life support. He was inclined to do so. Had it been my wife, I would have withdrawn support and let her pass peacefully. That was my mindset when I began to petition Heaven for the mercy to comfort Shelli's family and to allow her to die peacefully. A more benevolent influence took over my pleadings, first speaking words of hope, then promising miracles. The words from some other realm passed through my mind, promising Shelli she would recover and resume her activities as a wife and mother. To my mind, the promises were incomprehensible. I wrote in my journal, "It was almost as if Shelli were telling me herself."

Shelli's husband called back the next day to give me an update and ask my advice. I told him my medical assessment. It corresponded with his and with the experts providing care. Then I told him about my experience in prayer. I felt guilty for giving him hope or suggesting he should prolong the inevitable. He decided to continue care for a time. After the call, as I walked back to my hotel, the feelings I'd experienced the previous day returned. "I felt like Shelli was telling me she would be okay, and not okay in the sense of dying and being spiritually okay, but in the sense of being healed and having many years yet on earth with her family." I even felt impressions that she would bear another child and live to see that child grow up.

Sheila and I ended our trip early, and I got on a plane to go support my friends in person. The series of prayers and miracles that followed was beyond imagination. That she stabilized enough to transport home was a miracle in itself. When she arrived in the neuro-intensive care unit in Salt Lake City, every expert painted a grim picture. With her cardiovascular status now stable, her long-term prognosis was years or decades in a nonresponsive state. It was hard to imagine something more horrible.

Weeks later, one month after her accident, Shelli opened her eyes and began to speak. Everyone was stunned. I got the news via text while working in the ER. As thrilling as the development was, she still had a long journey ahead. When she started to take food, she developed severe abdominal pain and pneumatosis intestinalis on her abdominal scan. All evidence pointed to the ominous diagnosis of dead bowel. Surgery and extensive bowel resection was mandatory, but everybody was reluctant to subject her healing brain to general anesthesia. She needed an orthopedic procedure as well, but no one would do it for the same reason. She asked me to pray for her. As before, all my medical acumen was supplanted by some otherworldly promise that her surgery would accelerate her healing, that it would prove a benefit rather than a setback. The words made no sense.

In the OR, Shelli's bowel looked fine, no resection required. No one could explain it. While she was under anesthesia, they rolled her over and fixed the piece of free-floating pelvic bone that had likely caused ongoing injury to her brain by releasing small bits of fat into her blood stream (fat emboli syndrome). It was a procedure no one had wanted to do because of her brain injury. In retrospect, it seemed that some divine influence had given her the clinical symptoms and the scan appearance of dead bowel in order to get her into the OR. When she came out, her bowel was fine and her orthopedic problem was resolved. Exactly as promised in the prayer, the surgery accelerated her healing. She was awake and smiling before the end of the day.

A month later, Shelli was well enough to go home, but not without more problems. She'd developed a rare condition, forming bone in her soft tissues and around her joints. From all available medical literature, her condition was both chronic and progressive. Surgery was a potential intervention but risked making matters worse. The team took a wait-and-see approach. She again asked me to pray on her behalf then went home to continue her recovery.

That Shelli was alive and talking was a greater gift than anyone had hoped. The sorrow of learning she'd been pregnant at the time of her accident and had lost the baby was swallowed up in the miracle of her life and recovery. When she and I spoke about it later, we referred to it as her summer of miracles. In the weeks that followed, Shelli's x-rays confirmed that all of her heterotopic bone had disappeared, a phenomenon never before reported in the medical literature. To top it all off, little more than a year after leaving the hospital, she returned to give birth to her youngest son.

When I told Shelli I was writing this book, she sent me a note. "I remember the comfort I felt whenever you'd come to the hospital . . . I've always felt a special bond with you from the time I met you. I'm sure you made promises to me in heaven when I found out this was going to be a step in my journey. I'm sure you stepped up and told me, 'Don't be scared. I'm going to be there for you through it all.' And you were! I've always known if I needed something you'd do everything in your power to help me."

I was wrong on virtually every expectation of Shelli's medical care. I don't know if she was talking to me early on, telling me what to say in those prayers while she lay unconscious in a hospital bed in Hawaii—she doesn't recall any out-of-body experiences—but I am grateful that I listened and uttered prayers contrary to my earthly understanding.

I had to let go of my ego to accept direction.

23

BELIEVE

Spiritual experiences sometimes come to skeptics and critics. Sometimes they've come to me when I've been skeptical or critical. More often they come when I believe. Even if the experience is new or seems contradictory to what I think I know, I try to trust and go forward. I've been wrong; more often I've been led aright.

When I'm proud or impatient or arrogant, I'm alone.

Some say humans can't comprehend the infinite. I disagree. Imagine yourself in a spaceship traveling across the universe. Now double your speed. Now double it again. Now triple it. As you continue to travel, take a break to eat lunch and listen to your favorite music—something soothing or exhilarating, your choice—then come back to the window. Have you reached the wall yet? Whatever your speed, double it again, and again. Have you reached the limit of your infinite mind? No. Nor will you.

Ever.

What humans really fail to comprehend is the finite. We can't imagine a boundary to the universe or the end of our existence. The closest we can come is to imagine ourselves in a black box in the ground, or as a pile of ashes in an urn. But we still exist.

Try another exercise. Imagine yourself in the center of a large round room. Pick any spot on the wall and imagine you see there the beginnings of the universe. See the cosmos come into existence as the planets and stars take their positions. See as much or as little detail as you like. Hover there until you're satisfied and then scan to your right. As you move along the wall, see the waters flow, the volcanoes erupt, the first appearance of living organisms. It doesn't matter whether you believe the commonly accepted scientific explanations of the beginning of the universe or the traditions of divine creation. That distinction is not the point of this exercise. Just see the images, moving and living, within the context comfortable to you. See the pyramids, the prophets, the wars and inventions. Continue your timeline until you come to your own birth and the present day, and then go as far into the future as you wish.

Now you have a panorama of eternity, all flowing and active and in any imaginable level of detail. Reach your left hand toward the past and your right hand toward the future. Bring your hands in front of you, compressing the panorama until it's fully in view and you can see it all at once. Everything is still there. You can see it all as one eternal now.

Now zero in on the massive 1815 eruption of Mount Tambora in the Dutch East Indies. Look carefully. Expand that portion of the panorama until you can see the atmospheric debris and the year without a summer. See the yellow sunsets, the crop failures, and the widespread famines. Now step into the panorama and experience it. Live it and learn it firsthand. When you're done, return to the present and chose your next experience.

Here's my point: the human (not mortal) mind has no difficulty comprehending the infinite. Time and space are not the issue. I've looked into the future. I didn't like it. I'm not talking about the cataclysmic end-of-life-as-we-know-it future. I'm talking just a few months or several years. I didn't like knowing and waiting. I think if I asked I could see more, but I don't want to.

When I believe, I am more likely to experience. And when I experience, knowledge supplants belief. Believing opens the door to knowledge.

24

NEAR-LIFE

I've shared just a few experiences from a small segment of my life, mostly from the first year of my friendship with Jeff Olsen. I thank Rachel on this side of the veil, and Tamara on the other, for bringing Jeff and me together.

People ask what I've learned from my near-life experiences and how they've changed me. I would say this: it's not about what I've learned. It's about what I've lived. Learning is of little value without living. Living *is* learning.

These things I know: there is an omniscient, omnipotent, and infinite Creator who is, above all things, benevolent and forgiving and abounding in love. If that infinitely compassionate Creator is not omnipresent, then messengers, angels, emissaries, ambassadors, willing mortals, and untold other agents are. I am continually in the presence of Deity. And, on occasion, if I am willing, I can be an agent of that Divine Being.

We are more like our Creator than we realize. We are divine. When I shed my mortal veil, I see who I am and who my neighbors are, and I realize that we are all more alike than different. Our appearance may vary. Our culture and context may be widely divergent. Our concepts of heaven and eternity and God may conflict for now. But, when our spiritual eyes open, we are all alike.

I am here to learn to love others. I am here to learn to forgive unendingly and without reserve. I am still learning to forgive myself.

I know these things are true. I still struggle to live what I know, but that doesn't lessen what I know. I've struggled with things—the same things, over and over again—for decades. The struggle continues. I feel guilty at times, but when I'm near the veil—when I enjoy my most profound near-life experiences—the struggle seems irrelevant and the guilt is assuaged.

As I prepared this manuscript, the voice I've come to accept as an agent of my God said, "Let it go." I understood instantly the insignificance of my frustrating habits, but I wasn't being told to let go of my habits; I was being told to let go of the guilt. I could hear the judgments of others about the things with which I struggle. "It doesn't matter to me," the message continued. "Stop imposing other peoples' judgments on your life."

Jeff Olsen's near-death experience concluded with a probing question: "To what degree have you learned to love?" The question was as much about loving himself as anyone else. We all need to spend less time condemning and more time living and loving, even ourselves.

Several years ago, an elderly friend approached late one evening and asked if I'd come visit his wife. She was dying of pancreatic cancer. I'd known them both for years, and we'd talked about things that mattered most. She'd sent him to find me. We made arrangements and picked a day.

In their home, we visited at length. She'd been in pain and had rapidly lost weight. She and her husband both knew she would soon be leaving. Near the end of the evening, I felt impressed to tell her she'd shortly receive visits from loved ones who had preceded her in death. They would return to comfort and assist her. I could feel the unseen souls as I said it. I knew what was about to happen. I wanted to stay and experience it with her, but I knew it wasn't for me; it was for her and her grieving husband. The next morning, he called to tell me she'd been communing with deceased family members through the night. It all brought her great peace. She passed a few days later.

Sometimes it's the mortals who need a facilitator; sometimes it's the spirits. I don't know why either is the case or why it seems so inconsistent. When it comes to spiritual matters, I've found my frequent answer to be, "I don't know." I'm comfortable saying it. One thing I do know: when I've been willing to go, I've learned and been uplifted. I've always received more than I gave.

One last story: A deceased man came to me some time ago and asked me to deliver a message to his brother who was a friend of mine. Until that moment, I'd had no knowledge of my friend's deceased brother. I asked why he'd come to me instead of his brother. He said his brother wouldn't receive such a visit.

The next day, I delivered the message. I was hesitant, concerned my friend might be hurt by the fact that his brother had come to me instead of him. First he confirmed he had a deceased brother. Then he listened carefully and concluded the counsel had indeed come from him. To my surprise, he confirmed he wouldn't have been receptive to such a visit. He didn't explain why; I didn't ask. He expressed his appreciation for my willingness to be the messenger.

For all I know, the only reason that soul came to me was because I knew his brother and I was willing. Sometimes, just being willing to hear and act puts me in a position to experience eternity. When I do something for them that they cannot do for themselves, they reciprocate and do something for me that I cannot do for myself. I try to be willing.

25

NOT YET

Before concluding, I have to offer a moment of brutal honesty. After all I've experienced, I'm still afraid. I'm not afraid of death; I look forward to that. I'm afraid of the path through mortality. I know there's another step I could take if I just asked. It might be an easier step than the last one, or harder. I don't know what the next step is or where it goes or what I'll learn. I just know it's there and that there's no other way to get where I need to go.

The last time I naïvely asked for an experience, the blessing came gradually and painfully through years in the cauldron. Ultimately, the benefit proved worth the price, but it was wrenching and horrible and, at times, seemed endless. Twenty years later, I see with more perspective. The pain helped me. It allowed me to help others. Someday I'll find the courage and trust to ask again.

As I wrote the concluding pages of this book, I enjoyed a strong and persistent spiritual presence. He lingered over my shoulder for an unusually long time. His presence was so strong and so persistent that I became emotional and wondered why. Finally, I asked my two proven questions. In response to the first: "I am your brother." To the second: "Keep going."

That's what I'm trying to do. Keep going. The end is *not yet*.

LESSONS LEARNED

Quell Ego

Believe

Be Willing

Eliminate Fear

Breathe

Ponder

Ask

Listen

Feel

Write it Down

Trust

Don't Judge

Forgive

Serve

Touch

Practice

Remember

Share

Love

Keep Going

ABOUT THE AUTHOR

Jeff O'Driscoll, MD, experienced many shared-death phenomena and other spiritual encounters during his twenty-five years as an emergency physician in a level-one trauma center. He welcomed souls arriving into this sphere of existence and bid farewell to others who were leaving. Sometimes he encountered those who hovered between worlds. Having traversed the tenuous terrain near the borders of mortality, he now helps others understand the lessons learned in their near-the-veil experiences.

Dr. O'Driscoll recently took a leave of absence from emergency medicine to do consulting and to write. Many of the lessons he learned from his spiritual experiences are incorporated in his children's books, available at MucktheDuck.org, and his recent novel, *Who Buried Achilles?*, available on Amazon.

Dr. O'Driscoll obtained his MD at the University of Utah School of Medicine and completed his residency in Salt Lake City, Utah. He is board certified in internal medicine and is a fellow of the American College of Emergency Physicians. He has published works in theology, ancient scripture, history, medical science and medical administration.

In addition to writing, Dr. O'Driscoll enjoys painting, sculpting and cycling. He is a talented public speaker and loves teaching both small groups and large audiences. He and Sheila have been married for thirty-one years. They have five children and three grandchildren.

Made in the USA
San Bernardino, CA
15 February 2018